MRL

Tight lines & n
by the bank.

Love, Dad.

Love, Mum.

GW01463809

Fly Fishing

on

Still Water

Fly Fishing
on
Still Water

SIDNEY DU BROFF

MOONRAKER PRESS

FOR NEDRA,
COMPANION ON THE WATER, AND
IN LIFE . . .

AND FOR ALL OF THOSE WHO HAVE CREATED
FOR US OUR STILL-WATER FISHING. OUR
DEBT TO THEM RUNS VERY DEEP. I
ACKNOWLEDGE IT WITH PROFOUNDEST
THANKS, WITH A GRATITUDE THAT IS
EXPRESSED EACH TIME MY FLY FALLS ON
STILL WATER.

Cover picture by Nedra Du Broff

© 1981 Sidney Du Broff

First published in 1981 by Moonraker Press

26 St Margaret's Street, Bradford-on-Avon, Wiltshire

SBN 239.00199.0

Printed in England by T.H. Brickell & Son Ltd,

The Blackmore Press, Shaftesbury, Dorset

and bound by Butler & Tanner Ltd, Frome and London

CONTENTS

1

The man who taught me to tie flies gave me two lessons, then loaned me a book in lieu of a third. That was the lesson in which I had hoped to learn to make a muddler. 'The book explains it all,' he said; then suddenly I was on my own. His advice was to stay with the standard patterns, and to make each one over again until it was perfect before going on to the next. He had started me off with a Black and Peacock Spider, but I got tired of making them long before I made them perfectly. By the time Lesson Two was behind me, I had departed from standard patterns and I took to the deviationist path.

Over the years I have developed or evolved a large number of flies on which there have been some extraordinary successes, and which have provided enormous pleasure and satisfaction, both in their creation and in practical use. This is not to suggest that there haven't been plenty of failures, too.

Other of the flies have been given to me. Some are discoveries: while standard patterns elsewhere, they are not in common usage here. At least one I found, created by an anonymous tier, the barb of the hook broken off; when reproduced in similar and varying forms it gave consistent success during the season. Those marked with an asterisk (*) are illustrated, and appear further on in the book, in alphabetical order, complete with instructions for their creation. With these flies and with these methods you will probably catch more fish than before.

Obviously, nothing works all the time—neither fly nor method. Flies that took fish today, may not do so tomorrow. Yesterday is different from today, and tomorrow may be different still. The season evolves; new life comes into being. Flies are probably the most effective way of taking trout—and I am including live bait. A fly can be anything—a worm, a shrimp, a maggot, or fry, an insect—terrestrial or aquatic—in any of its stages of development—in any colour. It can even be a frog or a mouse. And into any of these artificial creations the fisherman can engender life, or at least life-like movement.

It is largely a question of determining what the trout are having or will have, sometimes apparent, but more often not. Are you offering them food, provocation, challenge, an object of curiosity? Any of them might work—or none. It is possible to be doing the right thing in the wrong place; unless we fish a water with a fair degree of regularity, we come to it each time almost as a stranger. It therefore becomes a question of finding out what will work.

Fly fishing is not an easy game, despite the occasional 'easy' success. There are no hard and fast rules to follow in order to achieve success, because if there were, you could follow them and always take fish. The fact that our still-waters produce something like one or two fish per man per visit is a pretty good indication of how difficult it is, particularly so when you stop to realize that those waters are stocked with 50, 100, sometimes 200 fish to the acre. It is the difficulty, the uncertainty, the challenge that makes the game intriguing and exciting, and the taste of victory so sweet. It is my fervent hope—and belief—that this book will contribute substantially to an increasing number of victories.

So come fishing with me—I'll tell you what I did—about my good days, and about my failures too.

2

I attached the *Pheasant Moth to the leader and cast it out on to the still water. It sank beneath the surface, and continued to move downward in the depths. This was at Weir Wood, in Sussex, on a hot morning in the middle of August. The sun shone brightly. I fished from a boat, anchored mid-water, maybe 75 yds out from the dam. The Pheasant Moth had never been in the water before. It was a new creation, now being used for the first time. It had a body of red and green chenille, pheasant feathers atop, lying flat, with free-flowing peacock herl tied in at the head. The fish would probably be down deep, in the cooler water, feeding on any of the number of things the dam trapped, brought here by the wind. Certainly nothing was showing on the top. Today would not have been considered ideal. But most of us, most of the time, have to take it as it comes, fishing when we have the opportunity, not when conditions are deemed perfect. All that we can do is adapt, be sufficiently flexible to alter methods as knowledge and experience would indicate.

Slowly, steadily, I retrieved the fly, attached to the sinking line. It did not take long before an answer came from below. a fish hit that Pheasant Moth hard. He was on—broke water and danced on his tail—fighting the way they did at Weir Wood. In due course I brought him in—not a big fish—one typical of the water, ranging somewhat over a pound. But would it happen again? It did, a short time later. Almost every cast produced a fish or a hit. The fly was fairly large, a long shank No. Six; perhaps they were striking it out of aggression, rather than as food.

By the time I landed my fourth fish the sun was really blazing. It grew hotter by the minute. Occasionally there would be a slight breeze, but not a cooling one. It was more like a desert wind. With the breeze, the smooth water would take on a slight ripple, which would die when the breeze did. The fish were taking as the fly approached the surface; but when I began the retrieve earlier, before the fly went deep, nothing happened. Apparently they were following the Pheasant Moth up, striking it when they thought it might disappear.

Popular fishing mythology has it that the fish won't strike when the sun shines brightly—and that you might just as well go to the pub. The fish haven't heard about this, though an amazing number of fishermen believe it, or at least say they do: maybe it's the rationale for going to the pub. Admittedly there weren't a lot of fish being caught that I could see; around me now there were 11 boats, here, I supposed, because of my own success.

Weir Wood is not an easy place to fish. It is moody and temperamental, it changes its face frequently, sometimes within minutes, at the behest of the wind. Its surface can be smooth as glass, broken only by the feeding trout that dimple the top, or it can turn nasty, in just a little while, with white caps lashing out in anger. It can be generous sometimes—selectively—and notoriously ungiving at other times. This lake had beaten me more than once. It takes knowing, and even then, almost as if it were sheer contrariness, shows still another side of itself. Then it laughs at those whom it has left in confusion. Yet, it is a beautiful, sparkling gem, here not because Mother Nature so ordained it, but because man wished it, and so made it. Weir Wood is in fact man's gift to Nature. Seeing it, who could believe it had not always been here? Around its 289 acres the trees show leaves that are all shades of green, from the lightest to almost black. When the wind blows, the leaves turn over, and some of them reveal an underside that is pure silver. A dove coos, a crow calls. Ducks are at home here. The water has a mystique about it, a mysterious quality that is felt, but that defies explanation. It is a living body, not just a mere receptacle for the storage of water.

Today Weir Wood had been kind. Today I had solved its mystery. But I understood it well enough to know that tomorrow it would probably present another mystery. The fifth rainbow grabbed the Pheasant Moth as it was sinking. Today I wound up with a limit, one of the three that were taken.

3

It was late in April, and already pretty warm. Here, in Hampshire, are the Damerham Trout Lakes, literally dug out of the ground by Colin Harmes. This was the dream he had created, and set a standard by which other still-water fisheries are judged. It was my first time down here, and I had some new Muddler Streamers; the question was, would they work? A number of other things I had tried didn't. It seemed to me that this was sink-tip line water; I wanted to get down, but not too far. The lakes are relatively shallow, with fair amounts of aquatic growth around the bottom. Normally the water here is very clear, making it possible to hunt fish and cast a fly at them. Today, uncharacteristically, the water was muddy and spotting fish was virtually impossible. Personally, I'm not a fish hunter; I like them to come as a surprise. Looking at the water now, it might easily have been completely devoid of fish, though I strongly suspected that it wasn't.

I switched over to a sinking line and an *Orange and Black Streamer Muddler, fishing from the end lake. It didn't take long to find out if it was going to work: it did. Within the first few casts it took a 1½-lb rainbow. Not long afterwards it took one that went 3 lb. 6 oz., followed by a third that almost made two pounds. When the Orange and Black slackened off, and the sun shone brightly, I put on a similar fly, but in *Yellow and Black. Almost immediately it was struck. The fish fought hard, jumping out of the water to shake the hook. On the third jump it succeeded. but it wasn't long before there was another one on, and this one stayed. That was my limit. Of the 11 people fishing that day, I wound up high man.

Not far from Damerham is Allen's Farm. The four lakes are rather small and somewhat claustrophobic, though the fishermen I encountered had no complaints. Only one of them had as yet taken fish, on a shrimp. The water was clear and weedless, and you could see a long way into it, though you couldn't see any fish. After casting various things for a while I began to wonder if the fish actually were there. But the shrimp man assured me that there were plenty of fish, but they were probably in the middle of the pool. He suggested that I cast out as far as I could, with something big and bright. I put on the *Yellow Bomber, on a sinking line, which hadn't taken any fish before. But now it did. Eventually it took three. When its effectiveness tapered off, on went *Dave's Hopper, an American pattern created by Dave Whitlock, on which I had not taken anything before. On the first cast, a figure-eighting it in, it was taken.

Getting local advice can often, but not always, be helpful. It can be a short cut to knowledge and information that might otherwise have to be discovered by trial and error, and may, in fact, never be discovered. A man stopped by to have a chat, a northerner who had taken up residence in Hampshire, and who showed me his collection of flies with great pride. They had started out in life as standard patterns, but as they grew worn from use, he had attached some feathers here, a piece of fur there, topped off, perhaps, with a muddler head. They were, the man assured me, very effective. They didn't look like anything I could identify, and the fish might have had the same problem, though this could be a decided advantage.

The next time down at Damerham was in August, and it was really hot. But the heat had not materially affected the fishing, and if anything, it was better now than it had been in April—at least for some of the fishermen.The temperature ultimately reached 93° in

Hampshire, and brought forth masses of little flies that no one in living memory had seen before. As it turned out, they were thought to be extinct, but in fact had only lain dormant, waiting for this moment when they could start feeding on me.

Cowering from the sun, I took refuge in the shade of a tree at the top of Mayfly Lake where, if the fishing wasn't so good, at least it wasn't as hot. I kept rubbing antiseptic cream into the fly-bites, but got no more than temporary relief; the scientists who had concocted this cream had not made provision for 'extinct' insects. The Welshman with whom I had talked earlier came over to see how I was doing. 'Not a touch,' I said. 'How about you?'

'I got my limit,' he said casually.

Fishing had started at ten. It was now 12:20.

'Actually,' he went on, 'I finished about an hour ago. I've been at the lodge having a cup of coffee.' His biggest fish went six-and-a-half pounds.

'What are you using?' I asked.

'Come on back to where I've been fishing, I'll show you. I'll give you a couple. You better stand there and fish. You won't get anything here. The fish are turning around and swimming back the other way before they get up this far. I can see them very well.'

He gave me two *Bronze Herl Nymphs, one with luminous red tail and collar, the other with luminous yellow tail and collar. Thus armed, I retreated to my shady corner, where, despite the magic flies, nothing happened. I'd have to endure the sun. Out I ventured, taking up the stand where my benefactor had once stood. The first of his flies I put up a tree and couldn't retrieve. Ultimately, with the second fly, I had a fish on, but it came off after a couple of seconds. Several times fish came over to have a look, but turned away at the last moment in what appeared to be disgust.

Around three o'clock a man came by bearing the load of a hefty limit, the biggest in the five-pound neighbourhood, taken on the top with a Daddy-long-legs. A couple of fellows I knew took up positions near me. In a short time the one was into a rainbow that went 2½ lb, and minutes later, a second, only slightly smaller. The other fellow cast his line not far from mine and almost immediately he was into a good fish, one that turned out to be five pounds. I attached a white nymph to my line, and cast it out with new hope. Close to shore a biggish rainbow almost collided with it, turned sharply and was off. It was getting toward evening now, and for me, hope was fading fast. When you don't think you're going to do it, you probably won't. I gave up the struggle.

In the hut where one weighs up one's fish (if there is anything to weigh) and fills out the record card, I wrote the word 'NIL' on mine. Here I encountered a man filling out his own card. He too had been on Mayfly Lake, for at least a part of the day, casting from the opposite bank.

'How was it?' he asked.

'I didn't get anything,' I said simply.

11

'Oh,' he said, his voice filled with sympathy. 'I'm sorry.'

I was sorry, too, but the way he said it made it worse. I had gone without fish before, and would no doubt do so again. Given enough time, I'd probably get over it, but now my failure seemed even more poignant.

Later, getting into my car, the man came over to me, a two-pound fish in his hands. 'Let me give you this,' he said.

I was touched. He did not want me to suffer the humiliation of going home fishless.

Afterwards, thinking about the disdainful manner in which the Damerham rainbows had regarded my flies, I realized that it wasn't anything personal. More than likely it was that antiseptic cream. Rubbing it into myself during the course of the day, I also rubbed it into my flies. While trout don't depend upon their sense of smell in selecting food, as some species do—they rely more on their highly developed sighting ability—their olfactory senses are fairly acute, sufficiently so to have been repelled by the smell of antiseptic cream.

4

The *Sika and *Sika Muddler are two flies that have produced some pretty good results. Their origin is the Japanese sika deerskin that hangs on my wall. It struck me that a thin strip cut from the white hairy underside could make an effective fly. As it turned out, it was. It performed at Sundridge Lake in Kent when virtually nothing else would, on a bright and sunny day in August, and may well have been taken as fry.

To the sika body I added a muddler head. This performed very well at Weir Wood, at a time when a lot of people were going home fishless. One man with whom I spoke, fishing from a boat near mine, told me that on four previous visits he had gone blank. When I showed my fish to Nedra, she asked, 'What did you take them on?'

'Sika Muddler,' I said proudly.

There was a loud silence as she considered the implication.

'Where did you get the Sika Muddler?' she inquired, suspicion in her voice.

I confessed.

She made me promise to refrain from snipping any more pieces from the trophy on the wall. And I would refrain, unless of course the need became acute, and I ran out of sika skin. But I'd had the foresight to take enough for a lot of Sika Flies.

I don't believe that muddlers are, generally, regarded as fry, at least by trout, although they are by those fishermen who derive righteous pleasure from denigrating them. Fry, incidentally, are no less natural than insects, but as far as I know there is no movement afoot to propagate the use of flies that imitate fish, to the exclusion of flies that imitate insects. It is the fish, in the end, who will have what they want, not what the fisherman insists upon giving them. There are no doubt those who derive pleasure from a particular approach to fishing, and no one wishes to deny it to them, but to endow it with virtue is merely an attempt to engender prestige where none really exists.

Muddlers have also been accused of being crypto fish-pellets. This is even greater nonsense, since for fish pellets to be gobbled they need to be splashed on to the water in handful-size quantities. The creation of the Muddler is a magnificent contribution to fly fishing. The deer-hair head probably represents a delectable insect, and since it can be made to take a multitude of shapes and forms, it will serve in many ways. It can be fished on the bottom, when nothing is showing, fast, slow, or in erratic jerks; just beneath the surface; or on top, since its floating qualities are very good.

5

From a boat, near the dam at Weir Wood, mid-season, in bright sun, I fished the *Black Wool Muddler and the *Yellow Chenille Muddler. I fished deep, and slow. Five fish fell to those flies. It made me high man at Weir Wood that day. Nine others took one each; three caught two, and one caught four; about 40 others didn't catch anything, which for that day at least, worked out to less than half a fish per fisherman.

Is the fishing more productive from a boat than from the bank? Sometimes. On big waters it provides access to areas that could not otherwise be covered. It also provides an opportunity for drift fishing. But those who are knowledgeable about a water will probably do better from the bank than someone with less knowledge fishing from a boat. My own preference, usually, is to fish from a boat, simply because I like it, because it cuts me off from the land and makes me a part of the water. I like the solitude that it can often provide.

There are, unfortuntely, some waters that do not allow an individual fisherman to take a boat out by himself. We must be glad for the management's concern for our safety (though the presence of two in a boat, wielding hooks that travel at 100 m.p.h. presents a genuine hazard) but common sense on the water, as in other things, is sufficient to ensure our continued survival. The danger is not so much on the water, but in driving to and from it, particularly at the end of a long day's fishing.

Grafham and Rutland are two places, and there are others, where this senseless and discriminating rule applies. The management of such waters is completely misguided, verbalizing a concern that has no application in reality. Were this to be otherwise, it would only be necessary to insist upon the use of life-jackets while on the water, as they do at Queen Mother, Datchet.

It is the dam at Grafham that presents the real danger, yet I don't actually believe that in the interest of safety it will be removed. I climbed on to it one day, from the shore, and moved along it for some distance. The water was rough, and looked unfriendly. The dam itself was rather slippery. In the process of removing my sunglasses from their case and putting them on, I dropped the case at the edge of the water. When I bent down to retrieve it—I slipped and fell into the water. It was like being in a sloping bath, with my back dry and my front immersed. I tried to scramble up to dry land, but I couldn't get a footing on the slippery concrete no matter how hard I worked at it. I tried to crawl on my knees, pulling myself with my elbows, but with all that motion I remained in the same position. I was neither frightened nor panicked, only damned annoyed at my clumsiness, and at being immersed and getting wetter by the second. I had fallen in on other occasions, but had been able then to pull myself out, or somebody close enough was able to lend a hand.

There were people further along the dam, a good distance away, whom I could see quite distinctly. Obviously they did not see me; if they had, they would have come to pull me out. In all truth I preferred not to be seen, not to be observed as a clumsy oaf in need of rescue. I'd find my own way out—if I could. It was no good trying to pull myself forward along the concrete; it was just too slippery and slimy. I put my left index finger into the crack between the slabs at the edge of the water, easing myself forward inch by inch, my whole body dependent on that one finger. But I could not get enough traction—and slid back down again. At least I had found what appeared to be a method. If only I could use a whole hand—or even two fingers. If only I could have used the fingers on both hands. A sealant had been laid between the cracks of each slab, and only where it had pulled away a little could I manage to squeeze in a finger.

I tried again, easing my body forward slowly, powered only by that one finger. I got my chest out of the water, a part of it on to the concrete. I lay there, as if trying to grip the ground with my chest, afraid that on that slippery substance I would go sliding back in. Meanwhile, my fingers sought another crack into which they could cling. There were none. I could only try to hold on to the sloping slabs with the flat of my hands. This I managed to do, and then to bring my legs up, pushing against the slime that lay beneath the water.

I got to my knees and moved forward; at least I was clear of the water. I stood up. There was a solid cement under my feet now. It felt good to be upright again. Most of me was pretty wet. I emptied my boots and ignored the rest.

6

Latimer Park Lakes in Buckinghamshire is a small water totalling 13 acres. Though attached, the two lakes are separate and distinct bodies. They fish differently, and what works on the Upper Lake won't necessarily work on the Lower Lake, and vice versa. You are usually casting over fish here, but that does not mean they are willing to take what you give them. The water generally fishes differently each time you fish it. The knowledge acquired on one occasion is often not pertinent on the next.

I had some good results on the *Peacock Eye Fly, the *Maggot Muddler, and the *Cinnamon Nymph. Another fly that enjoyed some success, at least until it fell apart, was one that I had bought in Poland. I didn't really expect much from it, any more than from the other Polish flies. Some of them were quite nice appearing, but generally very badly made. I don't know the Polish name for it—if it has a name—so we'll call it the *Polish Fur Collar.

If I am reasonably certain that I am casting over fish, and they are not taking what I've got, I gave them something else, convinced that there is something in my fly box that they will have. I don't see the point in flogging away with the same fly after it has been presented in all possible directions and in all possible ways without success. A new fly brings a new dawn. Admittedly, it is not the fly alone; presentation counts for a lot—the depth at which it is retrieved, the speed, the direction in relation to the wind. If one thing doesn't work—try something else.

In fly fishing I don't believe that patience is a virtue. On the contrary, I think that it is a liability. Fly fishing is not static. Something is always moving, even if it is only a nymph or dry fly moving with the wind. If when casting over fish they see what you've got, and obviously reject it, it's time to put on something else, or move somewhere else.

In the course of one day I landed eight fish—and changed flies 34 times. On two occasions flies that took fish earlier were returned to the leader after a considerable interval, and took fish again. It had been a hard day, and three fish was the maximum that anyone else had landed.

Two of my fish were browns. I was pleased to have them, but not more so than if they had been rainbows. The truth of the matter is that, though somewhat bigger than a few of my rainbows, they fought considerably less well. They made a couple of hard runs, then turned over and let me scoop them up in my net, unlike rainbows that fight to the very end. I don't support the popular prejudices in favour of the browns that suggest they are a more 'natural' fish. In the lakes where they are stocked, they are no more natural than the rainbows. Probably there are those who associate them with pleasant, clear-running streams, which creates such an idealistic picture, while tending to forget how small they were in their natural state.

The fact of the matter is, we have never had it so good, with new waters created over most of the country that did not exist before, stocked with marvellous fighting trout that will take a fly, and that at the end of the day we can take home and eat. The fish are there because they have been put there, and we know in what quantities. We are considerably less dependent upon Mother Nature and her whims and fickle ways, and less dependent upon the weather, too. Nature had not been kind initially, but man, in his ingenuity, has filled in the gaps, and as fishermen we are richer for it. We owe a large debt to all of those who have made our still-water fishing possible.

7

During the colder parts of the year fish metabolism is substantially reduced, resulting in a decreased need for food. As the weather grows warmer and the things that fish eat become more abundant, the fish's metabolism begins to increase, with a resultant need to eat. For rainbow and brown trout, the peak feeding temperature of the water is 60° F, with the range being between 50 and 65° F.

Water-temperature will vary at different depths and in different parts of the lake. It therefore becomes necessary to scout around with a thermometer attached to a line, preferably an old fly line, at which knots have been tied at three-foot intervals. By lowering the thermometer and counting the knots, it becomes immediately apparent what the temperature is at a given depth. A bigger body of water will of course present greater variation than a smaller one.

If the heat continues to rise, metabolism will begin to slow down again—Nature's way of compelling the fish to conserve its energy in order to endure such a crisis; at water-temperature of 80° F, trout start dying off. Oxygen levels are also a factor, and there are devices that measure this, though not usually required by fishermen. The algae in the water makes oxygen during the day and consumes it at night, but normally generates twice as much as it consumes.

During the times when consumption is reduced, the feeding that occurs is likely to be on smaller food items rather than bigger ones. Consequently , smaller flies will usually prove more effective than larger ones.

The barometer is also a factor. A sudden drop can have an adverse effect. One minute the fish are rising, and as the pressure drops, surface activity stops and they disappear, waiting out the storm in the depths. Rain won't necessarily turn off the fish, but may start them feeding in earnest as the things they eat get floated down to them. At Sundridge in Kent one day sudden heavy rain brought the fish up to the surface, racing about in a frenzy, and in numbers larger than many had thought existed in the lake. Casting out my Sika Fly, I landed two before the rain finally stopped and the fish returned to their more normal haunts.

8

The *Gloria Fly took a while before it became successful, which surprised me, considering the way it looked in the water. It had started off life as white, elasticated cotton-wool embedded with silver tinsel, and intended as Christmas wrapping. I found it on the living-room floor in the Los Angeles home of my sister-in-law Gloria, whose name, because of her contribution, will be thus perpetuated. My wife's cousin, Roselle, is also to be honoured in this way, since it was her olive-green marabou feather that I stole from the vase in which it, and others, had reclined—until I came along—and made from it the *Roselle Muddler.

The *Mickey Finn was also encountered, an American pattern of long standing that I bought, on which the occasional success was chalked up. The fly takes its name from the drink to which a sleeping drug has been added. Use this fly, is the implication, and you will be able to put the fish you catch on it to sleep.

9

The River Taw at Umberleigh in Devon was low. I took a dace. And then another dace. Sea trout are supposed to come to it—sometimes; but not now, it was too low. Some were trapped in a pool up river, they said. They couldn't get further up, and they couldn't come down. They weren't taking anything anybody threw in their direction—just milling around. I myself didn't bother going after them: I didn't need any more frustration.

I'm not keen on night fishing. When it gets too dark to attach the fly to the leader, for me it's time to stop. I like the total experience, which includes seeing all that is around me. But for others, it is a special challenge.

There were supposed to be brown trout in the river, too, though admittedly small. I didn't see any myself. That is one of the problems about fishing in a river; you are affected by so many things over which you have no control.

Fortunately, not too far away was Stafford Moor, an attractive still water that saved the day for a lot of us. It's well-run, with a good stock of fish, some of them fairly large. I saw the back of one, as it moved slowly along the top, that must have been eight or nine pounds. This appeared to be a time when flies with metallic gold bodies took fish best—it did not seem to matter so much of what the rest of the fly was made.

A somewhat unusual team of displaced river fishermen had found their way here—a man in his thirties accompanied by his mother, a lady of about sixty dressed in wellingtons, skirt, and gold earrings. Both were obviously accomplished fly casters, but neither fully approved of this still-water set-up for trout; if it wasn't actually immoral, it certainly was unnatural.

From the other side of the lake, in posh, though agitated tones, the son's voice could be distinctly heard: 'There's a rise, Mother! Cover it! Cover it!!! You're blind, Mother. You're blind!' When Mother continued to fail to cover the rises, the distraught son grabbed the rod from her hand and cast at them himself. Five minutes of bombarding the area with Mum's fly failed to materialize in a take. Still annoyed, he handed back the rod.

Toward evening what could have been the limit-fish broke me on the Black Wiggly Muddler. The manager who was nearby, said, sceptically, 'I suppose it was one of those ten-pound browns'.

10

The summer produced the usual successes and failures. When the fish were feeding close to the surface there were some good days with a floating line, greased leader, but with ungreased droppers. I can't say that I'm really keen about using more than one fly at the time on my leader, though there are plenty of good reasons for doing so. I feel that I'm relating directly to that one fly—that we are connected and that I can feel what it is doing, can visualize its movement in the water, as I stop it, jerk it, twitch it.

It was the first week in September. I had tied up a number of flies, in various shapes, forms and materials, and one by one cast them out on to the water. It was a pleasant day at Latimer—warm, but not hot. The sun shone, though not brightly. There was nothing much moving in the water, at least not conspicuously. That always seems to worry people—if they can't detect movement. The fish have not been swallowed up by the sea monster that inhabits the depths, they are there, feeding on something below. It is when they have been rising that I have experienced my greatest frustration. We have all been through it, when the water has boiled with fish, and when none of them would take anything we had to give them.

Now they systematically rejected all that I offered them, until I got to the *Teal Muddler, a gold-bodied fly with teal feather and white ostrich herl flowing from the head. On the first cast it took a fish. On the second cast it took a fish. And on the third. On the fourth cast there was a fish on, but it came off. On the next cast after that it was hit twice. But on the next, nothing happened. Had it gone dead, lost its power, its magic? I inspected the fly. The gold foil body had been vigorously chewed and now hung in pieces, the tying thread showing through. It looked to me like the Teal Muddler had had it. But since it didn't matter anyway, I cut off the hanging pieces of gold body and cast it once more into the water, hoping that if I retrieved it quickly enough, its imperfections would go unnoticed.

The fly was almost at the boat when it was struck. The fish took the Muddler down and ran, but he stayed only a little while before getting off. Well, at least the bare middle my fly was displaying didn't deter the fish. A cast or so later a brown took the Teal Muddler. He hit hard, fought hard for a short time, then gave up.

A man fishing from the bank almost opposite me asked what I was using. Muddler, I told him. He put one on, fished it for a bit, got a take—but lost it when the fish got away with the fly because it hadn't been tied on securely.

With my limit in my bag I relinquished the boat. The man from the bank took immediate possession of it. I saw him some time later anchored near where I had been anchored. But he took no fish. Just once he'd been hit. He gave the impression that it was my fault—that I had led him down the garden path and into what he thought was a magic boat that, when he came aboard, turned into a pumpkin.

11

About the middle of September the browns became active—fish that do not grow with the same rapidity as rainbows, and that ounce for ounce fight considerably less well. It was not a good day. It rained somewhat, on and off. Latimer was not giving much. But something had to be right, some fly, or flies, that I had in my box. The Teal Muddler had already taken fish—as it was sinking. Not much point in persisting with it. What else would they have today? There were a lot of things they wouldn't have.

Pursuing the concept that something should always be moving—I moved myself, and then the Orange Marabou Muddler, on to my leader. Made with a gold body, it had the nice action created by marabou. On the first cast it took a brown. And in due course it proceeded to take some more. With the exception of one rainbow, my limit that day consisted of browns—the only limit. That fly evolved from one that had produced fair success from time to time—a red floss body muddler, with silver ribbing, orange goat-hair, and pheasant tail tied in at the head.

Mike, the Bailiff, told me that one of my flies had been found—in the mouth of a rainbow that had broken me earlier. It was the *Mink Muddler and the fish had been landed two days later. The Mink Muddler had had its moments—a gaudy fly that can be effective in late summer. Made with double wings of orange and red, tied in at the sides, its body was of mink, though any similar material would probably serve just as well.

The Teal Muddler took a lot of fish, then during the middle of one day, went off. A man fishing from the bank reported that the fish were feeding on what looked like green caterpillars dropping from the trees that hung over the water. So that was responsible for the rises. On went a green nymph that got a fish first cast, but it came off. But a couple of casts later there was one on and that got landed.

I had my limit but decided to continue fishing, and got another day ticket; it was going to be easy now—I had the answer. But now that green nymph wasn't working, so off it came, and a small, light green nymph went on that soon got me a fish, which came off at the net. It might have turned out to be an extremely effective fly, but it was now chewed beyond recognition and couldn't be used any more. I went through a lot of green things—they're sometimes very effective late in the year. My fingers finally reached for a *Green Caterpillar that I had bought, but had never before used. Tied on a hook that had been bent to create a more life-like insect, it had legs that were created from golden pheasant feathers. In the water it presented the most life-like appearing caterpillar that wasn't a living, breathing one created by Nature herself, that I had ever seen.

It didn't work. A bright green seal's fur nymph took a fish. But that was all. The day passed and darkness fell and all that came to me was that one additional fish.

That caterpillar may one day take fish; perhaps there will come a time when only it will be effective, though I admit that I remain somewhat sceptical. However, because it was such a perfect creation, for better or for worse, here it is.

12

Linch Hill in Oxfordshire, a 54-acre disused quarry, stays open late into the year. On a cold day at the end of October I rowed about on the unfriendly-looking water. Soon it started to rain.

The bailiff said that the fish here started rising about eleven o'clock. It didn't seem to me that much would be rising on a day like this. But around eleven o'clock, fish began rising. He had said to fish the wind line—the point at which the wind strikes the water and creates movement. Though it is in an almost constant state of change, it nevertheless suggests an approximate area in which to fish.

It did not strike me as an ideal day. But someone on the shore took a fish, so obviously it could be done. The water-temperature was around fifty degrees. This was a day that called for small flies. I ultimately got around to using a tiny *Royal Coachman, an American pattern that I'd bought some time earlier, and that in America, at least, had proved highly effective. Today it did, too. In addition, the *White Herl Fly, made of white ostrich herl, did its part, too. On the first cast it got a hit. The fish was on; then it was off. A few casts later it got hit again, and this time the fish stayed on.

I dropped an oar-lock. It was easily done. They were not secured very well to the boat. It was plastic, and did not sink as fast as if it had been made of metal. I plunged my hand into the cold water and snatched it back from the depths. But next time it fell off I did not act quickly enough and the oar-lock came to rest on the bottom. I could see it, in what was probably three feet of water. But the current was so strong that it propelled me past the lock—I could not hold the boat still with the oar. I created instead a murky sea of mud which entirely obscured the oar-lock. In desperation I cut a piece of rope that happened to be in the boat, and improvised a lock, which worked adequately, if not well.

From out of the rain, the wind, and the cold, an angel appeared. No, I was not hallucinating, because she was a familiar angel, and she had appeared many times before. It was Nedra, clutching a white box. Inside there were apple slices, recently baked, from the bakery in Eynsham. Eating them hungrily, with hot tea from my thermos, life wasn't half bad.

The season ended. It had been a season of much joy. May the next one be equally so.

13

It was spring, or so the calendar said. But nobody really believed it. My ears hadn't read the calendar; they cried out for the flaps attached to my hat to be pulled down over them, to provide some protection from the biting cold. The flaps went down, the hood went up. A total of eight separate garments covered my back. I wasn't cold, but I wasn't warm either.

The wind was hard from the northeast. But up here at Queen Mother, Datchet, there was more of it, and it was harder. They had built this 475-acre sea up from ground level, a concrete bowl whose walls extended 66 ft into the air. Near Heathrow Airport, it was built to store water—enough to supply all of London's needs for a month—and nothing else. It was never meant as a place for trout fishing. But my friend John Noakes and I, and a lot of other people, thought it would be nice if we could come trout fishing here. The Thames Water Authority didn't think so, and made it painfully clear. But we persisted, and the Thames Water Authority changed its mind—allowing in sailors as well as trout fishermen—with everyone co-existing amicably.

For those who complain about concrete bowls, may I point out that they were built to hold water, and not to provide us with a place to come trout fishing. That we can do so is a privilege, and we must be thankful for the opportunity. Here at Queen Mother, they had a lot of difficulties to overcome; the banks were too steep to permit fishing, which meant the exclusive employment of boats. That, they felt, created other dangers, which they dealt with by requiring fishermen to wear a life-jacket provided by TWA. And to stock so much water with enough fish to make coming here worthwhile had to cost a lot of money. We had pointed out that Grafham Water was more than three times as big and managed to do the job adequately.

Now here at Queen Mother, the temperature was 38°. There had to be a wind factor too. And that made things worse. It was also drizzling. Today did not seem to be filled with promise. The water, some distance from the bank, checked out at 45°, at least five degrees below the level at which trout begin to feed in earnest. As expected, nothing happened here.

Eventually, I moved against the south bank, in the general vicinity of the inlet tower. I'd tied up a lot of new flies for this new season, but as yet none had got off to a very auspicious beginning. Based on the success of the teal muddler, there were new teal variations. It was the gold body, orange goat teal that really got them, though. Within a couple of casts I had one on that made me think that the Loch Ness Monster had transferred over to Queen Mother Reservoir. The fish stayed down there, not especially anxious to come up and swallow my boat, or even an oar. I was convinced that I must have some kind of record fish down there on my fly. It moved, in its own good time, this way, then that way, and showed no inclination of allowing itself to be brought in. There were, I knew, some big ones in here, and this, obviously was one of them. But I was wrong. It was a rainbow of no exceptional size— 2 lb. 13 oz.—a fighting fish every inch of the way. It did, however, turn out to be the second-best for the day.

The other fish came, on that same fly, smaller ones—two of a pound each; 1 lb. 9 oz., 1 lb. 13 oz., and two pounds. It had turned out to be a better day than I had thought it would. But a lot of people went home without fish. That particular type of fly stimulated the feeding/attacking process.

14

It may have been spring's intention to come, but winter wouldn't let it, and winter was stronger. The wind lashed the water, and Latimer, more like a wide river than a lake, was whipped into a froth. Normally fairly placid, white caps spent a good deal of April on its surface.The bad weather affected the fishermen rather than the fish. Those teal flies continued to be effective—almost too much so.

I used other flies—the Black Beetle, the Cinnamon Nymph, an

orange and black streamer; a fuzzy wuzzy bug made with pheasant feathers wasn't of sufficient interest to induce a passing trout to turn its head in the direction of the fly. And even a Teal Muddler without the herl flowing from its head didn't do anything. Obviously that herl was important.

There was some success on the *Skater when the fish were near the surface. It's an American pattern, not widely known, that has a lot said on its behalf. The claims might be somewhat exaggerated, but it no doubt has its moments. It's called a Skater, because that's what you do with it. The fly, with feathers wound around the hook, goes skimming over the surface of the water, driving the fish that see it into a frenzy, compelling them to chase after it. I must confess my surprise when I actually saw it happen.

The *Dub Head also took fish consistently, a fly with a silver body, a black, dubbed sealskin head, and a red feather on either side. A rubber body, with teal feathers attached, didn't tempt any trout that may have seen it while attached to my line. The fish were, as usual, selective, taking what turned them on, and ignoring the rest, even though at this time of year the selection tended to be somewhat more limited than it would be later.

One of our rods, Harold Coombes, a highly-capable and imaginative fly-tier, invented a plastic blood worm, that was wound around the hook, then unwound itself in the water, creating the impression that it was very much alive.

The fish were running about two pounds each, not bad for this time of year. Winter growth is usually limited, unless the weather is especially mild. As the weather warms up, the trout's metabolism increases. This results in a greater intake of food, now abundant. Growth is rapid, for rainbow trout are amongst the best converters of food into flesh of virtually any living creature.

The rainbow trout suits our still-waters extremely well, to a greater extent, in my opinion, than the brown. It is an infinitely better fighter, and certainly considerably less temperamental. The browns go in the water, and in many cases nobody ever sees them again. Their growth is slow, and they are a more expensive fish to produce. It is fishermen's bias—prejudice—that compels still-waters to stock them, which raises the cost considerably, and must in the end be passed on to the fishermen. Were the fisheries currently stocking browns to stop, they could probably add another rainbow to the bag without raising the cost of fishing.

Our Mr Henderson, the music teacher, who coached Kathleen Ferrier, is also a very able fisherman, constantly moving about the bankside. During a period when his wife was ill he took over the cooking, and we exchanged some recipes. He liked the pressure cooker for doing his fish—with wine at the bottom, followed by a layer of chopped onion, the trout on top of them, and lemon juice squeezed over the trout.

Nedra, who has never been very enthusiastic about pressure cookers, showed a decided lack of interest, which makes me think I ought to get my own. But there is a hesitancy about creating a rivalry in the kitchen, though we men take our fishing recipes with the utmost seriousness.

A couple of times the sun made an effort to appear. But it was more of a glare than actual sunshine. And the wind howled down on the water. I had a fish on; it was a good one, jumping all over the place. That was just fine, except the anchor wasn't holding, and the west wind was pushing the boat in the direction of the falls. Would I bring in the fish before I went over the falls? Well, actually I did, though there were some anxious moments.

By half-past-eleven I had my six fish (the four limit, with a two-fish extension) totalling 12 lb. 14 oz. Nedra wanted to picnic on the grass; was it not spring—late in April? But wasn't it also raining? Undeterred, she insisted—until it began to hail. Then we took refuge in the lodge, where all the others also sought sanctuary. Except, that is, for Harold Coombes, who, sitting in a boat in the middle of the lake with his friend, continuued to fish. A navy man, he probably remained oblivious to the heavy 'sea', now more turbulent than I had ever seen it before.

15

The rains that were already here continued to fall. At ten-thirty in the morning I entered the lodge at Latimer. A goodly number of the Tuesday contingent were sheltering here over coffee and tea.

'Got your four?' somebody asked.

'Six,' I said.

'I knew it!' Mike, the bailiff said.

'What's everybody doing in here?' I inquired, able to afford a bit of righteousness. 'You can't catch any fish from the lodge.'

If you're prepared for the rain it isn't nearly as miserable as when you're not. Waxed coats and overtrousers need the occasional rewaxing. And there is no greater blessing than a hood. It keeps off the wind and prevents the rain from running down your neck. If you can stay dry you can fish in relative comfort, and you stand a lot better chance of taking fish when you're on the water than when you're in the lodge.

The teal flies worked well on occasion. Often flies have their moment, and then stop being effective, for varying periods. Maybe they come back into their own next year, the year after—or never. It has a lot to do with what comes into existence around them, in what quantity, and when. There are, of course flies that seem to be able to take fish any time—though not all the time.

As I cast out one of those teal flies the line tangled. I proceeded to pull it in so I could cast again, but the fly got taken near the boat, just beneath the surface of the water—a two-and-a-half pounder. Mostly I used a slow sinking line. There was little surface activity, and one needed to get down, sometimes way down. Today they were not far under the surface. I'd let the fly hit the water, then begin retrieving immediately. I feel that with a sinking line one is able to exert more control, to keep the fly at the desired depth. whereas with a floating line, even on a long leader, when you retrieve the fly moves upward.

Today the Dub Head worked its magic for as long as I allowed it to do so. Then a sculpin did the rest. Of American origin, it was adapted to local conditions and reborn as the *Latimer Sculpin. Created with a peacock herl tail and a muddler head, it is an extremely versatile fly whose basic shape is very good. The body is white tying-thread, ribbed with silver, but can be made of foil in either gold or silver. It has been created smaller and larger, in brown, in black, in red, in orange. It has caught fish when nothing else would, and will earn a permanent place in anybody's fly box.

16

At Weir Wood, Friday the 13th was cold—but not unlucky. The sun showed itself as it rose, but a cloud came along and made that round sun into a flat-topped sun. In a boat, near the dam, I am bobbing around in the wind. Nothing much happens. I move about. There is a northwest wind. I try a lot of things that took fish before—but they won't now. What are they having? And where are they having it? All you can do is keep looking, and keep trying different things.

The *Teal Fuzzy Nymph takes one close to the surface, a fly with a metallic blue body, a teal feather wound around it. Have I got the answer? It doesn't seem to want to work any more. I bring it in fast, just below the surface where the fish happen to be, and it works. It works just fine, until it gets chewed up, and then the Dub Head brings in the final two.

It's ten-thirty in the morning, and for Weir Wood that's good. It all sounds so easy, and maybe people wonder if those who tell about their successes aren't leaving out the failures. Well, the next day, starting out with the same tactics—they didn't work. There are some hits, and a couple of fish on—and then off, and the sum total for the day was one ten-ounce brown trout.

17

It's the middle of May. It's also very cold. I've got two pair of stockings on and my feet are cold. The wind is coming from the east and the north, occasionally from the south and west: and sometimes from the east and west—simultaneously.The air currents meet, and they clash. I'm at Latimer, and I'm in a boat. It has an anchor, its own, attached. On other days, with variable winds, the boat has gone spinning around, its position changing constantly. But now I have brought my own anchor and between the two of them they hold the boat still.

The Dub Head takes one. It gets off. Never mind. It's a small one. The Teal Muddler takes one and it gets off, too. That wasn't so small. They're feeding—just below the surface. I'm using a sink-tip line. Only the occasional fish is showing.

Some Canada geese come by. They swim over to the boat to see what they can scrounge. They're not wild. I'm a sucker—okay, here's a part of my lunch. They take it as their due.

That Teal and Orange takes one that looks like it's over 2½ lb. It is, 2 lb. 10 oz. The Cinnamon Nymph—I haven't used it for a while; he's the one who comes from the knitting department at John Lewis. Do your stuff. And he does, too. By nine-fifteen in the morning it's another limit.

John Noakes appears. 'Brown nymphs,' I tell him.

He goes over to Neptune. I have some tea. While I'm having my tea somebody says. 'That chap over in the corner has taken three in half an hour.'

I look out of the window. The chap is John. By the time I've finished my tea and eaten a couple of biscuits, John is back. He's got four. John is a very good fisherman. Brown nymphs. He thinks we've got it easy here. He doesn't know about the hours of frustration, of dropping flies on water that never get a touch. What about the neighbour chap down the road who was here three times and never even had a pull?

18

Scotland—for the brave. Or the foolish. At least, this part of Scotland. But I don't know this yet. I will, however, be finding out in due course. This is the River Cairn, in Dumfriesshire. It costs four pounds a day to fish this water, which runs into the Nith, and the Nith runs into the sea. The haaf-netters stand in the Nith and snatch up the salmon as they come through. If there is anything to snatch.

They create the impression that there are salmon in the Cairn, but the farmer with whom I spoke never saw one; some sea trout, sometimes. It's the Scots revenge, the war against the Sassenachs, that they win every time somebody plunks down four quid for a day on their river. They, incidentally, pay eight pounds a year. *You* can't start until after nine o'clock—a good deal after nine o'clock. Tickets are available at the fishing tackle shop in Dumfries town when it opens (at 9:00 am) for the day of use only, and may not be purchased in advance.

I found the river, parked, and climbed into my waders. It's a nice enough river as rivers go. No fish, at least early on, but then as my mother-in-law used to say, You can't have everything. Making my way along the river I found a high bank with what appeared to be fairly deepish water below. I put on a white seal's fur nymph and cast it out into the depth. And what do you know? Eventually a fish came to it—one of those 'fighting' native browns for which Scotland is renowned. It actually made nine inches—the legal limit—but couldn't have weighed four ounces. I quickly threw it back, unable to conceive that anyone would wish to retain a fish that was so small. On a yellow nymph I got another one, of about the same size, and did the same thing with it.

A little while after that the baliff appeared. He was a friendly, chatty fellow, who didn't have much to do, anyway, since there weren't a lot of us fishing this water. How was I doing? Well, I wasn't too sure. Catching those fish was probably worse than if I hadn't caught any; at least then I could have gone on dreaming, believing that down there somewhere were fish bigger than I now knew were typical of the water.

'You don't mean people actually keep fish that small?' I said.

In reply he asked to see my permit.

'The biggest waste of four pounds in my whole life,' I said as he studied the permit.

He must have been laughing silently. They had my four pounds. There'd be lots of other suckers coming along with their four pounds, filled with hope.

'If you want some good fishing,' I said, 'come on down south—to England.' He probably thought I was slightly mad, but it was apparent that we had created better fishing than that with which they had been provided by Nature.

He glanced at my tackle lying on the bank, now some distance from me. 'Ach', he said, 'you want to be careful of your tackle. Some of the local lads have the habit of sneaking up and making off with it.'

It was nice to know that besides being in the land of tiny fish, I was also in the land of thieving kids. Even at our big public reservoirs in England, with easy access to all, thieving has not been a particularly acute problem.

Scotland is the land of the rainbow-trout-hater. The man at the tackle-shop blamed all their problems on it. Now there was actually somebody up the river breeding them, and what was more, he was taking all the water from their river to do it. But how in fact could he take it, and what could he do with it? Back to the farmer again, who explained things. The Nith is a tidal river. When the tide is in, the water does not flow into the sea, and as the water flowing in the direction of the sea has no place to go, so it backs up over the land and floods it, the tide holding it there. When the tide flows out, the water quickly drains. On the upper reaches they then complain about a shortage of water.

The bailiff advised the use of small dark flies. They didn't work. In the tackle shop they advised worms. Thanks, but no thanks.

19

Still in Scotland. I hate to be regarded as a suitable candidate for extremes of punishment. But here I was, a long way from our lovely created Southern waters, replete with fighting rainbows, in this land of brown tiddlers I'd be ashamed to put in my bag and carry home. But was this typical? Were there not some fighting fish in this mighty land with whom I might not ultimately engage in battle? I trotted along to the Information Office to find out.

Now we know that Information Offices are not always sources of information, especially information about fishing. Why this is, I'm not sure—since a place like Scotland spends a lot of money telling us poor southerners who have to put up with those hatchery-bred rainbow trout—raised on pellets, not especially big at three pounds—whose limited fighting qualities cause the muscles in our arms to ache as we struggle to keep them from breaking leader and rod—how good the fishing really is in Scotland.

It was amazing how little information they had at the Information Office. What about Dumfriesshire? What about some nice, natural lochs where the fish bred naturally, in water created by Mother Nature, there since before the Scots wore kilts? They didn't know. There had been some literature around on fishing, but there wasn't any now, and it wasn't their fault. Why didn't I go around to the Water Board and talk to them.

I didn't have anybody else to talk to, and nothing much to lose. I'd already been to the museum, so why not go along to the Water Board? At least the two young ladies with whom I spoke were pleasant. The husband of one of them was himself a fisherman, so she had a certain amount of sympathy for my plight. But no, there were no natural lochs on which I could fish. She was somewhat vague but gave the impression that although these natural lochs existed, and had been controlled by the Water Board, they had leased them to those who had made them private—and it was now impossible for me to aspire to fish on any of them. Why didn't I fish in the local reservoir?

I wasn't keen. But when I considered the alternatives, which consisted of a return trip to the museum, I put down my money and got myself a permit. They say you only get what you pay for, and that's what worried me. Because, for the dubious privilege of fishing for one full day on their reservoir, it was costing me one whole pound. If I resided within the Council area, the cost would have been only 60 pence. I could have a non-resident season permit for £7.00: for residents, the cost is £4.50. Seven pounds a season. What do you get for your seven pounds? Brown trout, and no bag limit. No rainbows up here—none of those horrible artificial fish in their waters—reservoirs.

Glenkiln Reservoir is about ten miles out of Dumfries town. It's a pretty place in a lovely setting—about 100 acres. I don't imagine that the 'native' browns in here had hatched in here, so presumably they had come from a hatchery, and had been stocked—just like we stock rainbows.

The place wasn't over-fished. Two men occupied a boat—the only one. There was a couple; a man alone; two people came later, stayed for a while, then left—and me. Perhaps if it hadn't been Saturday it would have been less crowded. Not that I crave crowds on the bank, but the dearth of fishermen suggested that it wasn't much of a place for fishing. I waded out in my chest waders. The men in the boat drifted toward me. One of them took a fish. Its size came as a shock; it was obviously less then the 8½-in. limit (200 mm—they've gone Metric over at the Dumfries and Galloway Regional Council) since he threw it back. I got a fish too. It was over 8½ in.—but not much. And then I got another one that was even less over the 8½ than the first. Ten of them would have gone a pound.

Fishing cross-wind, using the Teal Fuzzy Nymph, I got a hit almost every time, but the fish were probably too small to get themselves caught on what I would have thought was a rather small hook. The boatmen took another fish, but as far as I could see none of the others took anything. In the evening there was a rise, of sorts, but the fish were all tiddlers. This lot had a good deal to learn about reservoir fishing. Hopefully they will one day make the trip down to the South to find out. I don't think it is too likely, however, since their built-in antipathy toward rainbow trout will preclude the possibility of learning anything positive. Why do they dislike rainbows? I put it down to narrow-minded prejudice, to extreme insularity and isolation, to an antipathy towards change and a rigidity that has to cost them more money with less result than it would otherwise.

I believe that we are essentially better fishermen than they are, that we have a broader knowledge and understanding of both fish and fishing, aware as we are of the many methods and techniques that need to be employed in an attempt to take trout. They are rigid where we are, generally, more flexible. We'll catch fish in their waters that they'll never see, but employing their methods on our waters, they will catch far less fish than we will.

20

It was good to be back in the South, on our artificial water, with pellet-fed stocked fish. I'd been fishing since six in the morning and it was almost noon before I got my first rainbow. We had suddenly changed seasons, and the early spring techniques and flies were no longer operational. A floating line with greased leader, but with a sinking dropper took a fish close to the weeds that now covered a good part of Latimer.

The fish went for a peacock herl nymph that had always looked pretty good to me, but never until now very good to a fish. Neither did it, henceforth, ever look good to another. I ran through the flies; they—the trout—were feeding actively, and somewhat selectively, until I got to the *Grouse Tail Muddler. Made with a bushy tail of grouse and a gold body, it took a two-pound-four-ouncer on the second cast. Here and now, this was the fly that did the work, with two fish today over three pounds, bringing it in fast, on a sinking line.

Not far from me a man took two fish in 20 minutes, on a black muddler, moving it quickly through the water. Someone with whom I spoke later, and who hadn't taken any fish, complained to me that people were using black muddlers on sinking lines to take their fish. Yeah, well that was a pretty terrible thing, I had to agree. 'But it's kind of hard,' I said, 'to tell the fish what you think they ought to have.' Fish just aren't interested in what you think is the best method of taking them; it's more a question of giving them what they'll have. The man tied on a muddler.

It hadn't been an easy day, despite a lot of active fish. For me it had taken almost 11 hours to bring in my limit, not that I want to set any records for speed. Another man with whom I spoke, who sat despondent in the lodge, told me that this was his second year as a trout fisherman, and that he hadn't caught anything. He was, before this, a coarse fisherman, and a pursuer of salmon with shrimp and spinning tackle. But low water the previous year was responsible, he said, for the dearth of salmon, and the fact that he hadn't caught any.

That is the beauty of still-water. We control Nature, rather than the other way around. The fish are there, because they have been put there, and if we haven't caught them, it's our fault. And, if the fish haven't been put there, we'll go someplace where they have been stocked in greater abundance.

The man wondered why he hadn't taken any fish. Did he not have the proper flies for fishing here? He showed me his box. There weren't very many. 'Is this the lot?' I asked. It was. He didn't feel a need for a surfeit of flies. It is true that some people take all their fish on a very limited number of flies, a few of which achieve virtually all the success. It is not a technique that works for me. If they've seen that fly and obviously don't want it, I've got another one on soon enough: to put on a new fly is to be reborn. There is new confidence, a new hope. They wouldn't have the last one; maybe they'll have this. I am not patient, and as I said before, I don't think it's a virtue when it comes to fishing. So much of this fishing game is an expression of one's own personality.

Earlier, fishing from my boat, I had seen a man on the bank who cast with vigour and retrieved the same way, persisting for a long period. When he changed his position, I saw that he walked with some difficulty and used the long handle of his landing net for assistance. Later, I learned he was 89 years old. Does fly fishing contribute to longevity? I wouldn't be surprised. It sustains interest and provides physical activity outdoors. And the fish we catch, and eat, contribute materially to our health and well-being. May we all, at 89, still be on the bankside casting our flies.

21

I tied up 28 different flies—and none of them took any fish. The Grouse Tail continued to do well, but flogging away with it, or any other fly, for an extended period did not produce especially good results. I feel that they—the fish—like a change, to see something different. We have all noticed that often after a fly has taken a fish it will go dead and not take another. Conversely that same fly may take a limit in fairly short order.

Things are getting pretty rough as we went into July and the fish had an abundance of goodies from which to choose. What worked last time was a dead issue now; everybody was struggling. Fishing at Latimer, from a boat in the centre, surrounded by patches of weed, I scanned the surroundings for open water. There were fish here, which made me think that it could be a good place to be, though no one in the near vicinity was taking anything. I went through a lot of flies, and then, because I didn't know what else to put on, attached a little yellow thing that I bought some time before, had used a couple of times, and not again because it had never had a look in. It had a yellow hackle, with a gold body, peacock herl running down its back and becoming a tail—No. 10 short shank, which reminded me of a Jersey Herd, but wasn't. It was the *Little Yellow Killer. And that's what it did. Suddenly the fish were interested, I saw two coming after it. They were small, and they couldn't have my Little Yellow Killer. I jerked it out of the water before they could get it, causing, no doubt, immense frustration amongst the two fish. In a little while it was all over. Funnily enough, Mike, our bailiff, told me that the day before this area had been very heavily fished, due no doubt to the fact that so many fish were in evidence, and that none had been taken. Well, I'd had the fly that could do the taking. But yellow flies had never produced much by way of success for me. I went on to tie the identical shape, varying only the colour of the hackle, which produced immense success when a lot of other people were finding the going pretty rough.

Now, here, most of the time, I was finding myself using a sink-tip line. Though harder to cast, it puts, and keeps, the fly in a position that is often extremely effective. Not one for over-burdening myself with equipment, I nevertheless carry three rods with me. I don't always assemble all three, but there they are in readiness should the conditions warrant.

22

We celebrated Bastille Day by going to Weir Wood, which also happened to be Cousin Roselle's birthday—the cousin whose feathers I pinched. There is no connection here, though it would have been appropriate if on her birthday I had caught a fish with the fly created in her honour. But I didn't even use it.

Each time I come to Weir Wood, I am impressed by its beauty. Its image, that is always a part of me, is suddenly alive and real. This body of created water remains for me a constant mystery, with a solution sometimes—at other times the solution eludes me. The fish aren't big, but they are, generally, pretty hard to catch. This water, which has provided so much pleasure for so many people, was to be snatched away from us and made into a coarse fishery. I can think of nothing quite so debasing. There can have been no good reason for doing this, no justification. Those who loved this water fought hard and valiantly for its continued existence, and lost. The bureaucracy that wanted to kill it had the power to do so but it was a criminal act. I very much doubt that this water will succeed as a coarse fishery. But by the time this becomes apparent, it will probably be too late, and restoration may be impossible.

I got into my number fifteen boat and headed toward the dam. There was nothing moving. The fish don't have to be in evidence for them to be there. It was rather chilly, with a north—north-east wind. The temperature of the water at 18 ft was sixty degrees. But that bit of knowledge didn't help much, because if there were fish around, they weren't having anything I gave them. Suddenly the morning had disappeared. I'd better get some advice. At the lodge I spoke with Bailiffs Ken Sinfoil and Tony Miller. Ken said to drift fish, the way he did, using a short line. Tony said, 'Go over to the other side near the dam, and anchor.' He suggested a Silver Invicta on a floating line, and to bring it in fast. Two men—both highly knowledgeable—offered two different methods. Ken said he wouldn't fish any other way, except maybe in a gale.

I like drift fishing, too. It can be very effective, and sometimes it's the only thing that works here. Okay, let's start out that way and see what happens. A Dunkeld got a small hit. The barb was off the hook. Nothing else came along by being a drifter. We'll anchor—in that north-east corner, on the far side of the lake, in the shallow water near the dam. On went the Silver Invicta, and two fish fell to it. Then an American fly I hadn't used before—a *Silver Doctor, Size 14, with a silver body, accounted for another two. There were fish moving here. This area seemed totally different from the rest of the lake, an odd little corner that was separate from its surroundings, the water here tranquil, the wind subdued. From out of the reeds a family of ducks decided that they preferred to feed elsewhere, not in such close proximity to me, and swam off. But the half-dozen swans ignored me and continued feeding as if I were not there. The occasional grebe would pop up close by, appear to be startled, and dive beneath the water's surface.

Another American, the *Jock Scott, in Size 14, got me my fifth fish. Then a *Rainbow Muddler began to make its way through the water, its silver body as attractive, hopefully, as the others. It seemed at first not to have any takers, and I thought it was getting on to time for a change. Close to the boat, I stopped it. That's when it was taken. What started out looking like a bad day ended up being a good one, with a limit by five o'clock.

Perhaps if I had rowed around the lake I might have solved today's Weir Wood mystery on my own, but it is a lot of water to have to cover and in reality could not have been done. But today Tony Miller cracked the mystery for me. The fish had sought the warmer water, moving less here because the trees had created a barrier against the wind. The north-east wind would have blown the food to the opposite corner—the south, which I had fished for a time earlier, without success. The fish preferred the more settled conditions, with the warmer water, to the greater abundance of food, though things to eat for them were obviously not in short supply here.

23

I got back down to Weir Wood the next morning just after 5:30. By six it was quite warm. The day was sunny, bright and pleasant. At least, that was how it started. It was in complete contrast to yesterday. Fish were rising a short distance from the boat landing, and for a moment I considered fishing near it. But those rising fish seemed to be there to deceive me, to keep me from going back to that same north-east corner from where I had tasted success yesterday. I would not be deceived, I would go directly there.

Doubts began to arise, however, connected with that north-east corner, when I saw Bailiff Tony Miller rowing away from there. If the fishing had been worthwhile, he'd be stationary at this moment, firmly anchored. The water was smooth. The wind was from the south-west. I got over to my corner. Fish were rising. I wondered why Tony had left. I used the flies that had brought success yesterday, then I knew why Tony had left. I tried a nymph. That got me a half-pound perch.

The wind began to whisper from the east. The whisper became a shout. It clouded over, and got cold. The rises stopped, and nothing I dropped into the water was of the slightest interest to any fish that might have been about.

I weighed anchor, rowed out into open water, and drifted, Perhaps it would come on like yesterday. Give that north-east wind a chance to blow, and maybe in time there could be a repetition of yesterday. Out here nothing showed. The water was bleak and heavy, gentle Weir Wood wasn't gentle. On a sink-tip line I attached a series of flies that did nothing, either for me or the fish. I then put on my *Silver Pheasant, a silver body fly made with the feathers of a silver pheasant. In a couple of casts there was a fish on, one that went a pound and three-quarters—big for Weir Wood. Not long after that there was another fish on that fly.

Some distance up the lake there was another sheltered area, created by the rolling hills and a dense stand of trees. Though the surrounding water was heavy, here it was fairly still. I fished it for a time, hoping that this piece of tranquillity would produce some takers, but it didn't, and I continued to drift. Ken Sinfoil uses three flies on a short line. Tony Miller uses one, saying that more than that tangle. Ken doesn't like a sink-tip line—it's for a salmon on a river, he says, but here and now it was working. Fish Number Three fell to that fly.

After lunch I went back to that north-east corner. The surrounding water was heavy, but here it was calm. The occasional fish rose. The rising became more frequent. Ultimately the Rainbow Muddler went on, and today was a continuation of yesterday. Retrieving the fly, I stopped it near the boat . . . in due course three more fell to it. It was about 3:30. Weir Wood had smiled upon me again. Today, too, she had been kind. I had used the sink-tip line, though possibly another would have worked equally well.

24

Sunny, bright and warm at Latimer, and pretty hard going for some. Fishing from a boat, that Little Yellow Killer was doing just fine. It got three right off, from in between the weedy places, on a sink-tip line. It was happening too fast, so I put on the Skater, and skated it about on a floating line. They didn't want it, they weren't coming up to the top to get that sun in their eyes if they could avoid it. Okay, then what about a Little Red Killer? Fine, they'll have it. That's not such a great colour here, normally. Today it is a great colour —a three-pounder thought so. And the Little Green Killer? Why not? By 7:30 in the morning, for me, the day was over, with a six-fish bag.

But elsewhere it hadn't begun. Nymphs on floating lines weren't taking fish. I gave away my Little Yellow Killer; its magic was not confined to just me alone. And the Little Red Killer. Taking a walk along the bank, I encountered Mr Bingham, his line not visible upon the water's surface. 'What's this?' I demanded. 'Your line seems to have sunk.'

'Sinking line,' Mr Bingham confessed, caught out, but anxious to catch some fish.

25

We came upon Rutland Water suddenly. But we weren't prepared for it—glistening in the sun, daring us to deny that it had not always existed here. Rutland's creation is another tribute to man and his ingenuity. Its 3000 acres makes it the largest created water in Western Europe. That there should be mistakes in such a large undertaking was inevitable—and forgivable. But rather than admit to errors, they tried to cover them up with excuses and rationalizations that no one believed. The support that fishermen initially provided soon turned to outright hostility. Fishing records were anything but reassuring. A Rutland Water employee told a bunch of us at the bar in a local hotel: 'Word has got around, and people aren't fishing there.'

What happened? It was said that the fish stocked earlier devoured the fry stocked later. They did a test netting—and there were no fish in the net.

I had booked and paid for two days, but I had no intention of going back the second day. It was obviously a waste of time. Instead I went to Eye Brook, not very far away.

Eye Brook, on the other hand was a completely different situation. It is a 400-acre water, with no bag limit, but they let you know that if you have caught 12 fish, you have had a very good day, and there is a gentleman's agreement that fishing will end.

Boats are available to the single fisherman, unlike Rutland Water, though I had the pleasure of sharing one with a Lincolnshire police officer who came here regularly, and who the previous year had taken 100 fish from this water.

I was impressed too by the weed-cutter they use here; rather than attempting to do it chemically, they physically remove the weeds, employing a boat with a wheel-like device at the front that gathers the weed, which is deposited in the boat. They then dispose of the weed on shore and continue the operation. They also allow the use of privately-owned electric outboard motors. Their docking facilities are also unique, and practical. The individual, in the boat, cranks himself out into the water with the aid of a pulley arrangement, and upon returning, is able to crank himself in.

26

August is a funny month. You never know what to expect. The Little Killer bugs were still taking fish at Latimer—they were having orange now. I had a fish hung up in the weeds. He went 3½, maybe four pounds. The leader broke. After that I went on to twelve-pound stuff when there was danger of losing fish in the weed. The thicker leader didn't seem to make any difference to the fish, but it made me feel a lot more secure.

Mr Bingham appeared in a boat. Life is filled with surprises. I never expected to see him in one. But now it would appear boats had the edge, since you could pick your places in deeper water, less troubled by weed, dropping your flies into the clearer holes in the water. During this period, since boat fishing was more productive and not quite so frustrating weed-wise, there were more people wanting boats. One day I found myself fishing from the bank. I got a good fish on and he headed for the weeds. I couldn't hold him and just let him go for that cover. He got there all right, but it didn't matter—he was still on. I wasn't especially worried, since it was twelve-pound leader to which he was attached. In time I was able to bring him in—2 lb. 11 oz.

Sedge time is often opportune for using those fairly big, gaudy flies. This is particularly true if they're not taking the sedges you think they should be taking—namely yours. On the first go with that *Orange and Red Flame—a fly with a double set of orange and red wings set either side, and gold body—there was a hit. Second time, a hit; third time, a fish. I'd been throwing sedges at them without so much as a touch. They just weren't interested, and they were there in numbers.

Same thing with the *Silver Strand. That's a silver-bodied fly, made with white marabou, and peacock herl streaming from the head and tail, mixed with strands of silver lurex. On the first cast there was a fish. On the second there was a fish—but it came off. On the third—this one didn't come off. And a few casts later that fly was really hit hard. A fish out there took my line and kept going, stripping line from the reel. He raced across the lake, and stayed on the move, taking out line almost to the backing. But I brought him in—4 lb. 6 oz. There were my six—by twenty minutes past eight in the morning—totalling 14 lb. 9 oz. Funny how it works sometimes: not long before, I'd gone from eleven o'clock in the morning until nine at night without taking a fish.

The fish had been taken on a sink-tip line, the flies being moved fairly fast through the water. Though the day was dull, the white fly performed admirably, in this case at least, contradicting the concept of bright day, light fly.

27

There was lightning and thunder. It turned a grey-green-black and everybody who was in a boat got off the lake. Why, I'm not sure. Were there tidal waves at Weir Wood? I'd never heard of any and I didn't think it too likely, on a reservoir. But I got off, too, just in case—in case the sea-monster whipped the water into a frenzy. When I'd started out just after six in the morning, the surface of the lake had been like a glass and fish were rising in the vicinity of the boat dock.

Now the trees were silver, and the rain that fell was silver—like silver stones hitting the water. Eventually the rain tapered off, and the pervading greyness was not after all the signal for the end of the world—or even of fishing. Despite the disturbed conditions, Admiralty Wood, down the lake and protected from the wind, was fairly still. A limit could be had from here, casting a white muddler from a drifting boat, using a greased line, and keeping the fly on top of the water. Or a small *Deer Hair, made from natural deer hair, that one of the regulars was kind enough to give me. It looked like a sedge laying eggs on top of the water.

28

By the end of August you felt that autumn was on its way. About mid-morning I unbuttoned my coat—but not for long. Latimer generally fishes best early, but not always. It usually gets quiet at mid-day, not an unusual phenomenon, and then things might get active again towards evening. Might. Don't count on that evening rise. Not here, not anywhere. Sometimes it never happens. Sometimes that evening water is dead still, with nothing dimpling its surface.

An hour and a half went by without a touch. Then the Little Orange Killer went on, and got a hit first cast. It was a nice fish, that fish. It jumped out of the water and flung itself into the air—then jumped again. But jumping didn't work for him, and he just stayed down, swimming about, going around the boat, running, taking line. He didn't seem to tire; he didn't show any signs of tiring, though *I* was sure getting tired.

I brought him closer to the boat. He went out again. I could see him sulking there—a good-size fish I wanted a lot. Now only six or eight feet separated us—under the circumstances a very long distance. it could just as well have been a mile. There was no way of getting that fish in until he was ready to give up the struggle—to a greater extent than he now appeared to do. He towed the boat around in circles. My hand was numb. Then I saw signs of weakening—the first indication that I was winning this battle, though the battle is never won until the fish is in the net. This time I won. It took about 20 minutes to get him in that net, a fish that went 4 lb. 7 oz. and fought more powerfully than I had ever seen a fish of that size fight.

A large part of the day passed before I took my fourth fish—on an orange fly. Though there was nothing showing on the surface the fish grabbed it almost as soon as it hit the water. Would this technique work again? I cast out, let the fly touch down for but an instant and drew it back in, only to cast out again, and repeat the process. It was not a process that needed a lot of repeating today, because it took the next two fish in relatively short order. A bright fly moved fast along the surface sometimes works very well.

I tried to explain what I had done to a fellow who had come along for the afternoon, but the concept eluded him; it was not a part of his nature to bring that fly skimming over the surface for just a yard or two before casting it out again. He insisted upon a slow retrieve. It didn't work.

A couple of the regulars, fishing with nymphs, also went fishless. It's fine to have a favourite method of fishing—but it might not be the fish's favourite method of taking a fly—particularly at this moment in time. If you're fishing because you like the method—enjoy it. But if it's a case of trying to catch fish, it's better the one that catches them rather than the one that pleases the fisherman.

It had been a long, and rather hard day—a day filled with uncertainty, with a need to experiment, to change, to be flexible. My six fish totalled 16 lb. 9 oz. At this time of year there are often some fairly big fish around, having spent a good deal of the season eating.

The trout were fussy not only about the flies, but about presentation, an extremely important factor in taking fish. Sometimes they want it fast, and sometimes they want it slow; sometimes they want it in erratic jerks and hit it when it stops. The only way to find out is by experimenting, by constant change until you get it right. Sometimes it's that slow, steady retrieve that gets 'em. The wind is important, too. Casting with it over your shoulder is easier than casting into it. But a considerable amount of what those trout eat comes to them driven by the wind, since they—nymphs—have no means of propelling themselves outward. Casting across the wind is also effective, and at times the only way that will achieve success. Cast across, and slightly into the wind with a nymph. The point where it straightens out is often the point at which it is struck. But then there are the times when only the retrieve against the wind will bring a strike, often the case with streamer-type flies. One must be prepared, and able, to put the fly in all directions.

Last week's flies or methods often have no bearing on what happens this week. This week's fish weren't chasing anything on the top of the water, whether brightly coloured or otherwise. Funny how a fly works once, and though you keep flogging away with it, won't take another fish. It happened on a variety of flies today. And then for want of a better idea I attached the Roselle Muddler. First cast it took a fish. Next cast the fish was on for but a moment before coming off. There were several more hits, and then things went quiet for a time.

The action happened with the Roselle Muddler cast into the wind, and retrieved slowly. They wouldn't touch it if the movement was fast, but the slow movement made hooking them so they stayed on somewhat more difficult. However, here was today's answer. Here was something the fish would take readily. It got hit as I was allowing it to sink—by a rainbow that went 4 lb. 3 oz. Move it slow, move it steady. Hit. Hit. Then there would be a take. Today's bag of six totalled 15 lb. 11 oz.

29

The new season came, though most of us, around February, think that it's never going to happen. At Queen Mother, Datchet, I shared a boat with Mike Turner of Turner's Gunsmiths in Reading, a very pleasant fellow and a good fisherman. The wind whipped up the water, and it rained part of the time. You expect the new season to dawn with, if not trumpets blowing, at least the birds singing, flowers blooming, leaves appearing instantly for the occasion. But it's not like that, though when the fish are there, life is better, even if the boat is bobbing up and down so hard you have to hold on. At first they liked the *Moorhen Muddler, a black fly with a tip of white, and a silver body. But they also liked Mike's Black Chenille. And then they went on to the *Latimer Yellow Tail, so named because I'd bought it at Latimer (nobody knew what it was called). It had looked interesting, with its white-tipped black wing, and I knew that some day it would be the right fly. Today it was. But it wasn't all black that took fish today. A fellow tied up just opposite us, on the floating dock, was taking his fish on a Baby Doll.

At Latimer, when the east wind blows, it doesn't seem to make that much difference—to the fish anyway, though it does to the fisherman. I had a lot of new flies tied up for here. The *Gold Body Pheasant got hit right off, then started taking fish. The others wouldn't do, at least not here and not now. I went through the lot of them. Not a touch. They were holding out for the Gold Body Pheasant. Okay, have it—they did. But none of the fish was especially big, nor in the cold did they fight exceptionally well.

Mrs Arnold, one of our very good fishpersons, took a rainbow of 5 lb. 12 oz.

Instead of getting warmer as the days passed, it got colder, and I picked the coldest April day on record to go fishing. The ground was covered with snow. There was ice in the disinfectant troughs, ice around the fringes of the lake. The guides on the rod would clog up with ice and then I'd have to breathe on them and push the ice through. The wind was hard from the northwest, casting was rather difficult, and things were kind of slow. Fishing from the bank I'd managed to hang up several flies. The only thing positive was that despite the cold I wasn't cold—what with wearing seven layers of clothing.

There was a guy opposite, standing near the falls, taking one fish after the other. What on? Whisky Fly. Did I have one? I did, an original in fact. The fellow was passing them out to the less fortunate. He soon got his limit, and his benefactors began to reap a rich harvest. But on my Whisky Fly there was never a touch. His

Whisky Flies, I learned later, were tied by his wife. Obviously she tied some special quality into them, both unique and effective.

For me what got a limit today was the *Blue Body, a black fly with a blue metallic body. I encountered Geoff Gough, a keen Latimer regular who had already taken three fish. He wanted to start tying his own flies. The equipment was there, which Mike, our Bailiff, had thoughtfully provided, and now was a good time.

I'd do one first, as he watched. Then he'd do it.

'Which pattern are you going to make?' Geoff asked.

I was somewhat startled. Pattern? Pattern? I hadn't actually thought about a pattern.We'd just put it together and see what came out. What was in the box? That was going to have a lot to do with it. There was some black marabou and there was some silver tinsel, and some peacock herl. That seemed like a pretty good way to go about things. I did it and then Geoff did it. He learns fast and he's good with his hands. He tied up a very credible fly.

'Now take it out and catch a fish on it,' I said.

And he did, too—on the second cast, standing near the lodge, he got himself a 2 lb. 10 oz. rainbow. Thus was born the *Latimer Fly.

In the United States the Jock Scott is used as a trout fly, and very effective it is too. At least sometimes. I'd been throwing a bunch of the old favourites at those Latimer fish without getting so much as a touch. They obviously weren't favoured by the fish. But on that No. 14 Jock Scott, using a sinking line, and bringing it in slow, a rainbow grabbed it right next to the boat, within the first couple of casts. Between it and the other American fly, the *Quill Gordon, also in size 14, I managed a limit. It, too, was taken almost upon sight. The Jock is a colourful fly, while the Quill Gordon is rather plain. Today, as the cold persisted, they were probably showing a partiality to smaller flies. They didn't come all at once. The fish would go off 'em after taking one. I'd switch, or move, and then they would work all over again.

Poor Mrs Arnold, and a lot of the others, were close to freezing. It's hard to keep warm, particularly if you're sitting in a boat. Casting just isn't sufficiently active to generate much warmth. And you're getting, and keeping, your hands wet, in what is obviously some pretty cold water.

30

Lord Wantage has ten thousand acres in Oxfordshire, owned by his family since the middle 1800s. On the estate there is a furniture-making shop , a pottery, and various other craft enterprises. There is also a lake, created in a park-like setting, and stocked with trout by Lord Wantage, and meant for his use and that of his guests.

Today we can all be guests, for a reasonable price, with season rods preferred. The lake—Lockinge—is small, intimate, not very deep. Geese swim on its water, taking refuge on the island in the centre, ignoring the coots and the diving ducks. The beginning of the lake starts with a big pool that narrows down to a broad river. I always approach a new water with a certain amount of trepidation, as well as anticipation. What's in store? How to you fish it? What works best? What will work today? What works at all?

We arrived around eight in the morning. It was still pretty cold, but rather bright. I walked along the shore, looking, observing. Nothing moved. For no other reason than that I felt like it, I began to fish just past the island. I had some new flies today, flies in which I felt no profound confidence. The idea had come to me in a hotel room one day—that you could probably take existing materials from your surroundings and create them into flies that would take fish—curtain tassels, a piece of rug—my own shaving brush. I didn't actually depend upon the hotel for the supply of material, but limited myself to an old shaving brush and the brown and green portions of my own shaggy dog rug. The flies probably suffered from too many limitations; now that I think about it, an emergency that would require such drastic and dramatic action seems most unlikely. Well, I was fortunate in hanging one of those flies up a tree fairly early on—getting rid of it permanently. That still left me with a fair number with which I persisted then, and for some time afterwards, on other waters. I did actually take a fish on a brown nymph-like creation, which I suppose in a way proved my point, though I have to regard the entire experiment as a failure. I still have two of those flies left, but will get rid of them at the first opportunity.

So what did work today? The *Pheasant Streamer for one thing, made entirely with pheasant feathers. It looked quite good to me, though it had no early takers. Yet my confidence in it was infinite, or at least almost infinite. And in due course I was rewarded.

Using it, and the Chukar Fly, on a sink-tip line, I took my limit. The Chukar Fly is most interesting, and should have a bright future. Its origin is the chukar partridge, which inhabits the drier places of the world, a number of which I'd shot. The feathers have a double stripe running vertically through them, which struck me instantly as desirable fly-typing material. French partridge, game in England now, would probably do as well should the real thing not become available eventually.

We spent the night at a pub nearby, in Wantage, run by H. I. Samuel, a season-rod at Lockinge, and a man with fifty years of fly-fishing experience behind him, We exchanged flies—I gave him some Chukars and Little Killers, and he gave me various nymphs, which included the *Greyhound Nymph, invented by a friend of his. It's a very effective fly, Sam, as he likes to be called, assured me. You drop it into the ring of the rising fish. You can fish it fast, slow, or any other way—and it will be effective. I don't for a moment doubt it, though I must confess that I have never had a fish on it. But with Sam's strong recommendation, I have very great confidence in it, certain that one day I will take fish on it.

Sam was telling us about a visit he and two friends made down to

Avington. 'Between us,' he said, 'we had a hundred and fifty years of trout fishing experience. And you know something: we all went blank. But there was a boy—eleven years old—fishing right near us. He took four fish. None of them under seven pounds. That's fishing for you.'

Sam said that the ducks and swans were the fishermen's friends, that feeding in an area, they stirred things up, and trout came around to feed. A technique he used, either from boat or bank, was to cast out a white fly on a floating line, across the wind, then to strip out several yards of it after the fly had touched down, thereby creating a belly. Retrieve. When the fly, whirling around, straightens out—it may be hit.

A trick he's used at Blagdon was to row his boat around in semi-circles, in the shallow water where there was plenty of insect life, stirring it up, and inducing the fish to come in and feed. He then cast into the wake made by his boat.

31

Ron Irvine, just back from America, where he had fished at Lake Havasu, in Arizona, and where the temperature touched ninety degrees, complained of the cold here at Latimer.

'If you think this is cold,' I said, 'You should have been here in April.'

Ron is a good fisherman. Most of the time he uses a sinking line, maintaining that he is able to exert more control over the depth of his fly. Sedge pupa take a lot of fish and he doesn't change the fly often, but if nothing much is happening, he changes his place. Normally he prefers to fish from a boat, but does equally well from the bank.

For me, today was another American day: I took a three-pound, three-ouncer, on a *Parmacheene Belle, a red and white fly, number fourteen. Isn't that a lovely name—Parmacheene Belle. It's an old fly, developed early on in America.

The other one was a *Cardinal, a fly all dressed in red. I was particularly pleased about this fly because a Cardinal was the first fly I had ever bought, as a kid, long before I ever owned a fly rod. I saw it in a fishing tackle shop and wanted it. The rest of the stuff that went with it would have to come later. But it was a portent of the future. It was the way I wanted to fish, and it was an expression of that desire. Now, many years later, it was a Cardinal that took fish for me.

It rained, of course. It rained the whole day—with increased intensity. But Bill Mee, who is eighty-two, stood on the bank and cast his fly, completely impervious to the rain. And near him, Mr Henderson, equally indifferent to the rain, cast a grey nymph that had to be unique, since he had made it with hair cut from his own head. We all caught fish, too, while back at the lodge, fishermen sheltered from the rain. It isn't really difficult keeping reasonably comfortable in the rain with waxed coat, hood and overtrousers.

And back at the lodge, Tony Witherall told me about the fly on which he had taken a 4 lb. 3 oz. rainbow. 'When everything else fails,' he said, 'this one takes fish for me.' It's *Tony's Last Resort.

32

Church Hill Farm, at Mursley, in Buckinghamshire, was a recently-opened water, with two adjacent lakes of two-and-a-half and seven acres. Stocked with some big fish, it was already getting a good reputation. Early on I took a fair-size rainbow on *The Bleeper—an orange and white streamer. This gave me the idea things were going to be easy. I cut if off fast and tried some others. But you know, things weren't easy—things were hard. I moved around a lot and kept changing flies. Time passed and I began to wonder if there were any fish in the lake. To look at the water, you wouldn't have thought so. Owner Tim Daniels had said that the lake was over-stocked; he didn't like the idea of fishermen going home fishless, so he did everything possible to insure that it wouldn't happen often. But the fish couldn't be compelled to co-operate.

After the quietude of the afternoon, things began to happen, good things, like discovering that that Bleeper worked extremely well here. There was movement close to the shore some distance down from me. I cast at it and there was that fish on. The four limit averaged two pounds even—not bad for early on in the season. A fair number of fish were taken; one fellow, fishing with his father-in-law, returned for another day ticket, and wound up with a total of seven.

33

I found a fly. The barb was broken off. It was something like a Dunkeld, only it was on a long shank hook, quite big, and didn't have jungle cock feathers attached. I took it home and I thought about it. Here, I said to myself, was a kind of super Dunkeld, a Dunkeld the Martians might use, if they were fly fishermen. The basic tying had to be good, though it certainly wasn't necessary to stick to the same colour pattern. You could go off in hundreds of different directions, limited only by time and imagination. I went. The *Martian was operative. It worked at Latimer straight away, and it never stopped working in one set of colours or another. One of the most popular tyings turned out to be a green body with white feather streaming from the head.

That it was too good is no exaggeration. You had to be something to keep the day's fishing from being over so quickly. I put on a nymph that Mr Samuels—Sam—had given me, not previously used. I should have known that it would take fish—why else could he have had it? It did, then, and subsequently. Call it *Mr Sam's Nymph.

*The Snipe Fly was one I had made from the feathers of a snipe I shot. I used it quite a bit, but nothing much ever happened with it. A fly of that colour, with that action, had to take fish. Perhaps it just wasn't the right time. Its time would come. It did, and it will be worth re-creating and using.

The *Red Rubberband—a red rubberband wound around a hook—also took fish, though I must admit I'd had some doubts. On the American flies—*Rube Wood, and *The Professor—there were fish. And Harold Coombes gave me a dressing on which he'd had some good success at Queen Mother, Datchet—*Harold's Fly, a plastic body creation with a yellow marabou tail, fished close to the bottom.

Down at Weir Wood, things weren't so good, what with a strong wind having blown steady for the two previous weeks. You could take a couple off the top, and some from that north-east corner of the lake where it remained calm, and where there was a lot of activity. The Silver Pheasant worked, and the Silver Chukar. Bank fishermen were drawing blanks. But interestingly enough, over at newly-opened Bewl Bridge, not all that far away, they were taking fish, mainly from boats. But here the wind did not appear to be a factor. There is no doubt an explanation as to why some waters fish poorly when a north-east wind blows, and why others appear to be largely unaffected. But I don't know the answer.

At Queen Mother they had stocked with about 42,000 brown trout and after a while, with few of them showing up, they began to wonder what had happened to them. Had they died out, been eaten, or were they still there, having grown into something much bigger? It was a mystery for a long time, until they started to appear. They present a real challenge, though had they stocked with the same number of rainbows, fishermen would have seen many more of them. The technique Harold Coombes developed with the browns was to cast a fast-sinking line as far as he could, then strip out yards more, so that the line, sinking into the depths, would not wind up under the boat, to be hauled up as one would tie an anchor rope. The idea was to be down deep, but to keep the fly off the bottom. Queen Mother had come along very well, and was, without doubt, a real fishery. Another fly developed for fishing there is the *Silver and Gold, a fair-size streamer.

Latimer began to weed up. That could cause problems, but if you could manage to fish near the weeds without actually getting hung up in them—at least not too often—there were fish to be taken. From a boat the *Yellow Seal and Blood did well, and from the shore, dropping the Blue Muddler into the less-weedy holes took fish. But it was important to use a heavy leader. A hooked fish made for the weeds straight away. Another one, on which there was fair success, is the *Deer Beard, made with a splash of peacock herl and natural deer hair.

Mr Mee suggested to Mr Hopkins, who was getting into a boat, that a white Baby Doll with a yellow or green stripe down its back could be a productive fly today. Mr Mee was right, because Mr Hopkins took a limit on one like that. Mr Hopkins then advised Mr Coombes of his success, whereupon Mr Coombes, also fishing from a boat, hooked a nine-and-a-half pounder. It wouldn't fit into his net, so, brave man that he is, he held the monster's head above the water and slipped his fingers through its gills. 'I knew,' he said, 'I wasn't going to get it any other way.'

Alec Pearlman, creative fly tier and highly-skilled angler, a confirmed bank fisherman, upon hearing of Mr Coombe's success, proceeded to reserve a boat for next time.

I, not having a green or yellow-striped Baby Doll, went for the fly-tying box kept at the lodge, and with an existing Baby Doll, attached a yellow strip to its back, running from back to front. In a not-very-long-time, casting from shore, I took a 3 lb. 3 oz. rainbow.

34

I made the long-intended pilgrimage to Avington, a fishing domain that has become a legend in our time. Here I met the 'champ'. At least, he told me he was the champ. He held, he said, this year's record for total weight of a four-fish limit. It was considerably before starting time, which is nine o'clock, so he very kindly clued me in. Early on the fish would be along the shore. Cast parallel to it, left and right. As the day grew warmer, they would move into deeper water. Cast straight out. He himself was a fish-hunter—casting to those he could see. But not today—the water wasn't clear enough to see very far into it.

He stopped at the first lake. I went on to the middle one—it called me. Like he said, cast parallel to the bank. A Black Martian took the first one, as the fly was sinking. A Green and White Martian took the second. I had cast off to the right, was retrieving slowly, on a sink-tip line, when something went streaking past, a short distance from the bank, and parallel to it. Suddenly there was a fish attached to my line.

The day had started off hot, with a blazing sun, and every moment it grew increasingly hotter. By now my boots were off, and I was barefooted. I removed my shirt, wore only my waistcoat, afraid of what the sun would do to my exposed arms. It was just past the middle of June. A week ago it had been bitterly cold. Well, the heat didn't seem to be having an adverse effect on the fishing.

Now I started to cast straight out, into the deeper water, on a sinking line. I let it go down to the bottom, and there it stayed for a bit. Almost as soon as I started the retrieve it got hit. It stayed deep, unwilling to come in, unwilling to let me take back much line. It moved at its own speed, depending upon its sheer hulk to get its own way. I had the feeling it was big. When at last it showed a part of itself, I saw that my feeling was right. My heart, always surging with hope, now had the added effort of beating with increased rapidity. That was a big fish out there, and I wanted it, aware of the ever-present danger that it would get off the hook. Well, it didn't. I sighed with relief and pleasure as I scooped him in my net—an ounce-and-a-half under seven pounds.

The fly was the *Salt and Pepper, a nymph created from black wool, dotted with white, that had come from the knitting department of a department store. I stowed the fish away, along with the other two, in my cold bag, having to form him into a semi-circle to get him to fit.

Mid-day the Parmacheene Belle took number four. The three smaller fish went: 2 lb. 11½ oz., 3 lb. 3 oz., 2 lb. 14½ oz.

The heat lasted for but a day, there, obviously to torment me. Now we were back to cold June and cold July, windy, rainy. The fish weren't quite sure how to react to it all. The Martians worked well, the white nymphs, the green nymphs. I acquired a Caterpillar, a nice caterpillar, that when it tumbled through the water looked as real as any live caterpillar ever had. The fact that I never had anything on it should not be a deterrent to its creation. Some day it will be the right fly. The *Cork head, did, however, take fish, riding the water vertically, wired at the bottom to make it do so.

Over at Church Hill, I tried out more of those Martians, in a variety of colours. Within the first two casts I took a fish on the orange one, another on the red and white, and though I hadn't thought it too likely—a rainbow hit the Purple Martian hard stripped out line and spent a lot of time jumping out of the water. I played him to the net but he got off when the hook broke. That purple wing had started out white, belonging, originally, to a swan. With a Magic Marker I had coloured it. The results were unsatisfactory—the fly appeared to be rather unpleasant from a colour point of view. But then, it was really the fish I was trying to impress. A regular at Church Hill told me that he'd had remarkable success once with salmon on a purple fly.

Later, since the fish were obviously down, I let my black fly rest on the bottom, then brought it upward, where it was hit soon after it began to ascend. It's a technique that works well when the fish are feeding on the bottom.

The American flies in Size 14 took their share of fish. The weather remained cold. On 18 July I put up my hood to protect me from the wind. The fish were affected one way or another, but didn't follow any particular pattern. They'd feed for a while, then with a sudden change in the wind or drop in the barometer, they'd go off. You had to look for the fish, and the flies that worked before didn't necessarily work now. *Alec Pearlman gave me a brown and white nymph that had its good moments, often when nothing else worked.

Rigidity, always the enemy, was even more so now. You had to move about; if the fish weren't in one place, maybe they'd be somewhere else. If they didn't like one kind of fly, maybe they'd have another, or a different technique. By now the choice was fairly broad when it came to things to eat, and what they might have in this moment, they wouldn't later on. One man with whom I spoke told me that he'd taken two fish early on, one almost immediately after the other. If it was going to be this easy, he thought, his day of fishing would be over not much after it had begun. So he stopped fishing, drank some coffee, socialized, ate lunch, and ultimately went back for the rest of his fish. But he never got them.

Geoff Gough took a couple on a Damsel Fly Nymph. He gave me one. I got a fish on it and lost it, then lost the fly. He gave me another one, but they wouldn't have that one. Nearby, from the shore, Joan and Geoffrey Miller came for the evening rises that never materialized. A delightful couple, keen and competent fishermen, they always used floating lines, and often a dry fly. Pure as the driven snow, they resisted my best efforts at subversion. Not that they didn't do all right being pure; Joan took two rainbows of over six pounds.

A couple of times I put a fly rod in Nedra's hand and tried to show her how to use it. Two things became immediately apparent: Nedra didn't really like learning to fly fish, and that I wasn't a very good instructor. It brought home to me the importance of having someone competent to provide that instruction. It doesn't necessarily have to be a qualified teacher, but somebody who can communicate what has to be done, and how. Nedra grimaced fiercely as she endeavoured to get the line out, and not to wind it around the rod. She took the position that fun should not require so much effort, or so much learning.

But that's the fun of it—the new learning that comes with each new encounter. We learn from each other—like the Chinese say. Everybody has something to contribute. One imaginative tier created a Sweeney Todd with a big head by winding the tying cotton into an enormous ball, giving it three coats of varnish and painting on a set of eyes. It worked for him with great success.

35

The trouble with natural fishing is that it's natural. Nedra and I went down to Exmoor in Devon. It's wild and isolated, and uncomfortably overcrowded—since large numbers of people crave to go somewhere wild and isolated. We went to a hotel that claimed to have fishing, with a couple of miles on the River Barle. It was true, as far as it went. The hotel itself wasn't bad, and mealwise nobody could complain. But while they did have the exclusive fishing rights, they didn't have the exclusive swimming rights. I found a pool that held some fish—five-inch browns—fish natural to this water.

But then came those who would share my pool—a man and his wife and their three young daughters. They did not want to fish in it—they wanted to swim in it. For how long could I deny them their pool, as they sat patiently, looking longingly at the water? The Barle, known to be a fair river in places, is not known for its good fishing around Simonsbath.

But thank man for Wistlandpound—a still-water, naturally, of forty acres, not far away. You walk in, put your money in an envelope, and start fishing. The limit is six, and if you catch anything under ten inches—keep it, though it won't count as part of your limit.

Wistlandpound fishes best early and late in the day. Zulu and Baby Doll do well here. But a man staying at the same hotel as we, took his fish on a yellow muddler—mid-day.

I really should have gone back to Wistlandpound, but I got side-tracked. What happened was that Nedra and I took a walk along the River Lyn up to Watersmeet. We have this system where I spend a day fishing, and the alternative day doing whatever Nedra would like—walking somewhere of her own choosing; driving off to some village, looking at things, and then maybe going off to another village, perhaps stopping for tea. It's what I call my day for being 'miserable.' In all truth, I'd sooner be fishing, but I have to admit I'm not all that miserable on my day to be miserable.

But that's how I got side-tracked—onto this salmon thing. It was Nedra's day and Nedra, stopping on the bridge over the Lyn, said to me, 'I just saw a salmon jump.'

'I don't believe it,' I said, not even bothering to walk out onto the bridge to glance in the direction in which Nedra had reported what she thought might be a salmon.

She shrugged. 'Something jumped.'

I went to the centre of the bridge and waited and watched. And in a little while a salmon did jump. And another, and another and another. Five within a very short time—unless it was only four, with one of them jumping twice. I thought the poachers and netters had got them all. But apparently there were still some left. It was nice to see them. I'd given up the salmon game earlier, fed up to the teeth and thoroughly frustrated—as well as broke. Somebody said you had to be in good with God to take salmon. I wasn't.

The banks were lined with fishermen wielding spinning rods. Let them, I thought, feeling superior, since I had no intention of even making the effort. Then, just beyond the town, somebody took a salmon on a gob of worms. It could be done.

'Maybe you want to try,' Nedra said.

Maybe. We dashed up to the Angler's Corner at Lynton, run by a Londoner who wanted to get away from big city life, who thought Wistlandpound was the most rewarding place of all to fish. I got a licence that cost £4.50 for the day—a far less good value than the day ticket that costs £2.00 at Wistlandpound. The salmon had been waiting at the mouth of the Lyn for it to come right. Now it had, and they were moving up this spate river at great speed. They weren't stopping to linger, either. I moved along the bank, dropping a fly here and there, and finally came across this narrow place, about fourteen feet across, casting my fly up, and letting it come down.

The salmon were here all right—we saw somewhere between sixty and eighty—jumping high out of the water. One almost hit me, coming from behind as I stood on a jutting-out rock. Perhaps if I had been at the top, where the salmon would finally come to rest, I would have stood a better chance. But that is in retrospect—and who knows.

It was nice to get back to Latimer, and fill my mind with trout rather than with thoughts of salmon—so close and yet so far. At the Angler's Corner in Lynton I'd bought several flies, made probably by a local tier, for local consumption, but here and now extremely effective. One was called the *Owen, or something sounding very much like it; the other was what I thought the man said was an *Olson. Henceforth this is what they are called. The Olson had its moments, but the Owen had a lot of them. I took a limit by 9:30. As far as I could tell, twelve other people had three fish between them by that time. The flies had to be cast, not directly into the wind, but to either side of it. Dark flies, I told all I encountered, better if they have a touch of red at the front. Later, walking up the lake, two people were into fish simultaneously, and before they could land them, Mrs Arnold became the third, a three-pounder she let me net for her.

Twice I got broken, on consecutive days, with Martians. Once it was the Green and White, another time, the All Black, made now with a red wool tail and pheasant tail feathers serving as a set of antennae. It got taken the moment it hit the water, and that was the last I saw of it.

I went through a lot of nice flies, flies that I had created and in which I had put high hopes. But more often they were dashed. It made the successes sweeter, more delicious. One day, out of ideas, I put on the fly Mr Hopkins had given me some time before— the *Mr Hopkins Fly, naturally. The fish couldn't keep off it—a simple fly, made with peacock herl for a body, with yellow seal dubbed for a thorax. One of the fish took it so hard I had to cut the fly out of its mouth.

Some days they won't touch a winged fly. A simple *Black Seal dubbed nymph worked for me—and frequently afterwards. It was a fly that took fish consistently, though not all the time. The *Cream Seal also did okay, a dubbed seal fur fly that I'd made some time before. It had its times—not that they came around all that often. But on the Lower Lake, at times during August, it was just what they wanted. A man fishing near me, and reaping frustration, saw a daddy long legs walk onto the water and get himself devoured. He took the hint, attached one from his box—and saw it get taken first cast—by a brown that went 2½ lb.

Ron Irvine brought a guest. Henry Nichols, soon to become a member, who had just returned from a fishing trip in New Zealand. On a fly he bought there, whose name he did not know, and which I could not identify, he took a limit in fairly short order. *Henry Nichols' New Zealand Fly had an orange body, and red hackle. We don't know what it was, but it sure worked well—two of Henry's fish were over four pounds.

What worked for me was a *Palmer Chomper in white, this beginning of September. It can be tied with any number of variations, and all of them are going to work at some time or other. The fish go on 'em, and then off 'em. It had nothing to do with what's hatching. Each day and each week and each month brings its own new things with it, sometimes later than last year, sometimes earlier, and sometimes hardly at all.

Take Barn Elms—concrete bowls—yes. Sterile—never. It lives. It engenders life—in the heart of the city. Here exists not just one lake—but four. Take your pick—it caters to all tastes—coarse fishermen included. They have their water. There is the boat lake, the bank lake, and the any-method lake, all together, laid out as if a four-square draughts board.

From the boat lake, cast out in any direction—toward the Admiralty Building, Earls Court Exhibition Centre, the Television Tower off Tottenham Court Road, the British Airways Building, the Chelsea Football Field—and you could catch a trout on a fly.

The swans like it here. So do the ducks. Why else do they stay? If they have noticed it's a concrete bowl, it doesn't worry them much. The midge pupa like it just fine, and the sedges hatch as anywhere else. The boat lake does well on midge pupa, on a floating line. But keep those eyes on the line; the takes are barely perceptible. A lot of the regulars fish it this way, having come to know the water well. Or a rubber nymph—one man took five. They're highly selective, these trout on the Barn Elms boat lake. There is no shortage of things for them to eat; pull up your anchor, and if you bring up weed, it will be replete with shrimps. Not bad for a concrete bowl.

They had gone off those White Palmer Chompers at Latimer, and showed a decided preference for gold-bodied muddlers. Mrs Arnold took four in just a little while. The day had started off with a lot of surface activity on calm water, and they were having my Yellow Seal and Blood with alacrity. The wind came up and put a good ripple on the surface, and the fish went down.

Today wasn't easy. For some it was pretty tough going, though the big fish made their presence known—one over eight pounds and one over nine. I got broken on a gold-bodied muddler, but managed to land one on another—that went 3 lb. 11 oz.

Geoff Gough had one on that he said went over seven pounds. But it got off. Later, Henry Nichols, fishing not far from where Geoff had fished, got one that went over seven pounds. Was it the same fish? Geoff went back to see if there was another one. If there was, it didn't oblige.

36

Bewl Bridge is a 770 acre body of water that makes you think you must be on a Canadian lake. Besides the fishing, there is sailing, canoeing, rowing, diving, and nature trails around the lake. It also, incidentally, stores water—6,900-million gallons of it. Its maximum depth is 97 feet and its perimeter is fifteen miles. It was stocked with 87,000 brown trout and over 70,000 rainbows. The fishing had to be pretty good—and it was.

Where on this massive lake did you start, and on what? I started by asking Ken Sinfoil. He thought the south bank was pretty good, and perhaps the west arm—on an amber dubbed sedge pupa that had enjoyed a fair amount of success—the *Bewl Bridge Fly.

I had a boat and motor, a good way to become familiar with a new water, though there is always a danger of spending too much time moving from place to place, which is time not spent fishing. It's part of the learning process; what is it like over there, beyond that point, in that cove? It is the natural desire to explore, to discover, to set eyes upon pretty things that have not until this moment been seen before.

The big and sturdy boat cut through the water—no silly policy here of denying one man one boat. The day started off being drizzly and grey. There were Canada geese on a slope near where I anchored, and another slope covered with barnacle geese not far away. Right off I started getting hits on that amber sedge pupa, but no takers. By lunch time I didn't have a single fish.

When the drizzle died away the wind came up strong and I took refuge in Goose Creek cove, which looked like it would hold fish, but failed to produce anything for me. Later, in a somewhat protected area, I took four fish, one of them a brown, in fairly rapid order, on the Black Seal, the dubbed nymph. The brown was not noteworthy for the struggle he put up. Though a larger total number of browns had gone in here, they weren't showing to the same extent as the rainbows, and never would.

The next day I was back in the same place, with the same fly, and took a fish early on that slipped the hook at the net. For a while I fished in the area of Rosemary Farm, near the secondary dam at the east end of the lake. It was windier than yesterday, and while the anchor held, the back of the boat went swinging back and forth. I took a rainbow on a Yellow and White Martian, but this wasn't the most comfortable place on the lake.

Moving up a bit, to what could only be described as a corner, where the currents came together, I took another on that Black Seal, and still another—which happened to be an eight-inch pike.

The morning passed. In the afternoon I returned here, convinced that there were good numbers of fish here, as well as having some shelter, provided by the shrubs and trees. I searched through my box and I wondered what they would have. My eyes fell on a fly that I hadn't used before, one that I had bought at Lynton in Devon; a fairly big, white and orange marabou wing, with a silverish body—the *Collector, I call it, though the creator might have another name for it. It did not seem to me to be the fly for here and now; nothing indicated—from the flies that did take their interest—that this one should get any attention. But on the first cast it collected a nice 1¾ lb. rainbow, fairly good for this water. A few casts later it collected another fish. Then got a hit, followed by another fish that was on and off. The body began to unravel, but I made some emergency repairs and continued taking fish on that fly.

When at last it was time to go, I started up the motor. But I wasn't going any place. The motor roared. The boat drifted helplessly with the current. I wound up across the channel, on the opposite bank. Obviously there was something wrong here, something that had to do with the complete lack of propulsion.

I beached the boat. A man nearby was just packing up to go, having just taken his limit. Where, I asked him, was the nearest telephone. I'd call the lodge and ask for help. It would be getting dark soon, and I was at the far end of the lake.

The man looked at the motor, a little Japanese job, and said, 'I've got one just like that, only a bit smaller.'

He looked at the motor, inspecting the propeller. 'It's the split pin, I think,' he said. 'Stay right here. I'll go up to the car and get a pliers and see if I have any split pins.'

In a little while he was back, carrying a whole tin of split pins in various sizes, as well as other bits and pieces.

I hadn't remembered hitting anything with any amount of force, and certainly the motor had been functioning just fine when I turned it off earlier, prior to anchoring. Perhaps it had suffered a jolt, which had damaged the split pin, but which allowed me to go on for a while longer. Now it was completely broken and functioned no more. However, the man into whose hands I drifted, selected the correct split pin, installed it, and the motor was once again functioning normally. A bit of luck, considering that with fifteen miles of shore line on which to get beached, I chose the one on which a man stood who had a similar outboard motor, knew how to fix it, and had the tools and part with which to do it. I want to thank my anonymous benefactor. I hope we meet again some day. May he take many more limits.

37

Church Hill early in October presented all sorts of problems, such as strong winds that whipped the little lakes into white-cap-covered bodies of angry water; rain, clouds, sun and variable temperatures. The wind came from the south, pushing a lot of what would be dinner up around the north part of the lake. From the dam at the south end, there were plenty of people fishing, but none of them getting anything. Today called for a high degree of flexibility. If a particular fly or technique doesn't work, try something else. Nor is there a single technique that will necessarily be the answer for the whole of the day. Each of my fish came on a different fly. One of them was an Orange Martian, fished closer to the top than the bottom, moving it fairly fast. It was a day when the fish were taking short. Early on I'd had two on—and off. Today that had happened to a lot of people fishing here. The fish wouldn't stay on the hook, not having hit it sufficiently hard. But by moving the fly fast—they hit it hard and stayed on. The fish that were actively feeding were doing it in the northern half of the lake, waiting for the edibles to come their way.

Bewl Bridge set a record for the number of fish taken from any English reservoir—over fifty-eight thousand. They probably hadn't meant for so many to be taken, but it made a lot of fishermen happy—ageraging something like three fish per fisherman—and it gave Bewl Bridge a pretty good name.

I went back there toward the end of October, with my friend John Noakes. We had agreed to meet at six. A minute or so before that I arrived. John was ready. The six o'clock chimes sounded. Off we went. It's a hard drive, crossing the city. It might be early when you start, but not when you arrive.

I suggested we fish near where I had been marooned and rescued, from the shore, Ketley Pond way. You park on the road that crosses this end piece of water. The wind was coming from the west. It was almost summer again. There were sedges laying eggs on the water, and fish were feeding.

John didn't want to cast into the wind and so moved down aways. I don't mind casting into the wind if I think I might get a fish by doing it. And if I do happen to get a fish—then I'm delighted to cast into the wind. I got one, on that Black Seal, within ten minutes of starting. Then I got two more on that amber sedge pupa—the Bewl Bridge Fly. Number Four got the fly, but I failed to get him.

John, not casting into the wind, didn't have any fish. Come back, John, and cast into the wind. John joined me. So did some other guy, fishing a lot closer than good manners would permit. He took a fish in a little while, played it, and lost it at the net. He gave up, saying he was sick of casting into the wind and went away. The funny part of it—there wasn't that much wind. As far as I could see, the lot across from us, fishing with the wind over their shoulders, weren't taking any fish.

An amber sedge got me another fish—one with a fly already attached, one constructed in part with amber seal, and monofilament feelers. This fish was obviously a sucker for amber. The fly—let's call it the *Seal and Peacock—is rather interesting, and having been attacked by one fish, may be attacked by another, though here and now it took no other.

John started taking fish—on a green nymph and an Ace of Spades. In a little while he had four. I lost two on that white fly with the lime coloured back and tail. It was already pretty late in the day before I managed those last two. They took that Black Seal again. For me it's time to go when you can't catch the fly with natural light. But John persisted. I offered him my Black Seal. He declined with thanks. Unfortunately no more fish came to him.

I had thought this would be the last outing of the season. But the beginning of November was nicer than a lot of the days in August. And, as it happened, Barn Elms was still open and would remain open until the last day of November. Now, that isn't bad, is it, to have a fishery fifteen minutes from your home that opens on the 15th March and provides 8½ months of fishing, for not much more than three pounds, and allows six fish to be taken.

Today I decided to fish from the bank. I got there shortly after seven. There was a heron flying. He settled down on the railing of the stew cage, then eventually onto the base, waiting patiently. But for him there was no reward. The ducks moved from one water to another. The wind was blowing from the west. I cast across it. On the third cast I got hit on the Black Seal. The next three fish came on an olive seal nymph. And then after that things went fairly quiet.

Other people came, but they weren't taking any fish, despite my having revealed to them the secret of my success. Then the olive seal went quiet. In the next hour I gave the fish a wide variety of things from which to choose, and they didn't want any of them. Then I put on a small pheasant tail nymph. It's a pretty good fly and a lot of people catch a lot of fish on it, though it has never been particularly effective for me. With it, in a very short time, I had two on and two off. But at least here was a fly they would take, the re-creation of something they were interest in having. They were obviously being highly selective. Not only were they particular about the fly they hit, they were also fussy about the way it was presented. If it didn't appear natural, they wouldn't touch it. On a sinking line I'd cast out, across the wind, slightly to the right, not letting the fly go down too far. It would get hit at the point where the current straightened out the leader.

The limit came, and with it, the end of the season. It was a nice way to end it.

38

The season that ended at a Thames Water Authority Reservoir began anew at another one—Farmoor—in Oxfordshire. It was beginning its second season, and had, in the first, established a good reputation. Farmoor and Barn Elms, between them, had accommodated fifteen-thousand trout fishermen. This was my first visit here—and not a very nice day for starting out. Once on the motorway it began to snow—and snow hard—in blizzard proportions. Suddenly you'd drive out of the blizzard, advance a couple of miles, and you were back into it. By the time we got there the snow had turned to rain, and by starting time—nine o'clock—the rain had stopped, but the wind was blowing hard.

It was also Press Day, slightly over a week before the official opening day. For the occasion I had tied up some special flies—aren't all flies special flies?—made from wood duck feathers,

54

a bird we had encountered, shooting in Georgia, USA. These are the erratically striped, black and white, wing feathers, of which there are only a few. You look at them, and your hands itch to tie them into a fly. They are a common-enough duck in the United States, and their feathers are now available in Britain, though finding them may take some effort. However, the search is worth the effort. I was hoping that today they would be my secret weapon. They were—and I will reveal all—though another also performed well.

The first of the secret weapons was the good old Martian-style tying with wood duck wing. The fish wouldn't stay off it. Early on I lost the fly. Was it such a day that anything would do? Well, for one thing, around me there were not that many fish being taken. And second, I put on the Black Seal to find out. They wouldn't touch it. Then out came the *Big Gun. This was an intertwined black and white wool bodied fly with a wood duck wing tied streamer style. Naturally, on the first cast it took a fish. And then it took others.

Today, being a special day, the limit was twelve. By 12:20 I had them. I wanted time to wander around taking pictures and chatting. The other secret weapon that made it possible was the *Secret Weapon, a black and yellow chenille-bodied fly with water-hen wing tied metuka style. These flies worked well early on in the season, went off later, but had something of a revival toward the end. There is deep satisfaction about using a fly that has lain dormant and now suddenly again takes fish when nothing else will.

As is generally the case, presentation was important. I cast the wood duck flies into the wind, let them sink about three feet, and retrieved them slowly. They would be struck closer to the bank. But a short cast would not produce a hit. Nor would they be taken on casts made sharp left or right, while the Secret Weapon was most effective retrieved against the current.

For a while the sun came out and it was fairly bright. if not actually warm, though off in the distance there was an ominous black cloud, moving toward us. It was a nice atmosphere, with generally obliging fish, and who could ask for more?

On my travels around the bank I encountered a man whom I had met before, probably on a bank somewhere else. Why he was here, I am not quite sure. Because he wasn't very happy about it. Virtually with his first breath he told me that he normally confined his fishing to rivers and streams. His usual stream was one he named with a tone of superiority, but unfortunately it was all wasted on me because I had never heard of it. He also fished on the Spey for salmon, he told me. But he hadn't caught anything. For him, obviously, more important than catching anything, was being able to say he went salmon fishing on the Spey. So big deal, a lot of people go salmon fishing on the Spey—I've done so myself—but if talking about it is the sole reward, then we are all better off fishing at Farmoor.

How was this salmon fisherman doing at Farmoor? As a matter of fact, not very well. He hadn't caught anything. Close to the bank the fly would get caught in the weed, which gave him the distinct impression that a fish had actually attacked it. But the weed that he brought up at the end of the fly created some doubts in his mind.

He changed the fly for another.

'What are you using?' I asked.

He shrugged with indifference. 'It doesn't matter. Anything will do here.'

But he was wrong. 'Anything' wouldn't do. The fish weren't remotely interested. The fly was a red streamer creation which I could not identify, and which obviously had no application here. I left the poor fellow to contemplate his days on the Spey, still hoping that a fish, considerably less selective than the others, might come along to take his fly before it got caught in the weeds near the shore.

The cloud that was coming, came. The sky turned blue-black and the hail pelted down.

At Barn Elms not long afterwards, there was ice on the bottom of the boat. For a while it grew warm, then turned dark, with the rain coming down hard, accompanied by lightning and thunder. And then it turned bright again. April is filled with hope. Sometimes it is fulfilled. You can endure almost anything if the fish are there, obliging occasionally. They took black and they took orange. They wouldn't have the same fly twice. You keep changing, flies and techniques. Five came in the course of the day. The sixth eluded me. You can't complain with five.

It was nice to get back to Latimer. The greetings were warm and friendly and genuine. It had been a hard winter. A long winter. But it was past now. There was the future—a whole new season at which to look forward with pleasure and anticipation. We had come to know each other over the years—friendly, helpful, but most of us, essentially, loners. Only Mr Romaine was missing. He would not be fishing again. He would be missed—a quiet man who loved every moment that his hand held his rod—a man who took the deepest pleasure from a fish he could catch on a fly.

Mr Mee, now 83, had a couple of fish early on. Every opening day, he said, was good, and the weather, these past five openers, always satisfactory, so he knew that today it would be, too.

Harold Coombes, fishing from a boat, took four fish in an hour. Alec Pearlman, on the other side of the lake, fishing from the bank, spent 2½ hours getting his. There were fish rising today. Ron Irvine said they were browns, rising in the same place, in what was their territory. Mr Hopkins got four in a little while.

I was in no great rush today. Let me revel in the pleasure of being here. The fish—they would come. Let me savour the pleasure of the return. Today they would take my *Coon Tail—made from the tail of that dead racoon I'd found laying by the side of the road in Georgia, And they'd take the *Woolly Worm, from America, that you could wind in all manners of colour combinations, with maybe one of them being right.

56

TYING THE FLIES

Sid's Discoveries and Du Broff's Dependables (see pp. 61, 65)
The hook sizes recommended are those that have been successful, but if the tier requires bigger or smaller flies, there is no reason why he shouldn't tie them that way. In fact, multiplicity of sizes will no doubt contribute substantially to success.

Waxing the tying thread, particularly at the beginning and toward the end, will strengthen it greatly, reducing the chance of breakage. Buy the bee's wax at the chemist's, which requires no heating.

Wind the hook shank with copper wire, or similar, which may be purchased at the electric-goods shop, in large reels. Flies will sink faster and to a greater depth more quickly.

May the creation of the flies described here provide you with great pleasure and great success.

American Flies — The Lucky 13
These are standard American patterns, long used in the United States, for the most part, on eastern streams. The Jock Scott and Silver Doctor, salmon flies in Britain, are, tied on a twelve or fourteen hook, used as trout flies in the U.S. They are effective on British still waters.

New Zealand Flies
Use hook sizes of your own choosing, to suit conditions under which you fish.

The Salt Water Nine
Salt water fish are usually less selective than trout, often taking flies that suggest other fish. Silver is a good body colour, but other metallics do well, too, at the right time and place. Keel flies are often useful where weed is a problem. The hooks—a No. 2 long shank sea hook is about right, or a 1/0 salmon hook. They should generally be tied with copper wire to make them more sinkable, since they may be dealing with tides and current.

S D	=	Sid's Discoveries
D D	=	Du Broff's Dependables
Am.	=	American Flies
N Z	=	New Zealand Flies
Salt	=	Salt Water Flies

1. ALEC PEARLMAN NYMPH: Tie a strand of gold wire at the bend of a No. 8 hook. Dub cream seal's fur three-quarters of the way along the shank toward the eye. Wind the wire over the body in six,

approximately even, segments. Dub on a light brown seal's fur to eye. Create a throat hackle with a dozen light brown cock hackles of varying size, the longest reaching the barb of the hook. (*SD*)

2. BEAVERKILL: About a dozen grey mallard or teal feathers for the tail, approximately three-quarters the length of the hook. Thin gold wire for ribbing. Wind the shank with white floss. The hackle, brown cock, is palmered, taken to the tail. The wire is wound forward over the hackle to the eye. The wing is grey Canada goose feathers or similar. (*Am*)

3. BEWL BRIDGE FLY: Tie a dozen pheasant-tail feathers onto the bend of a No. 10 long-shank hook. Tie in a strand of silver tinsel. Dub in amber seal's fur and wind forward toward the eye, covering about three-quarters the length of the shank. Do not cut it off at this point. Bring the wire forward, creating the rib. Tie in pheasant-tail for making a wing case. Wind the amber seal fur forward to eye. Tie in a throat hackle of half a dozen pheasant-tail feathers, extending well back toward the barb. Tie down the wing case. (*SD*)

4. THE BIG GUN: On a No. 10 long-shank hook tie a half inch long tail of teal or mallard in generous proportions, or the comparable part of the feather in wood duck. With entwined black and white wool, wind the length of the shank to the eye. Take the black and white fringe of a squirrel tail in a generous quantity and tie it in as a throat hackle, long enough to reach the barb. Take the wood duck wing—hopefully you have been able to get some; this is the part of the wood duck that goes from being like that of the teal to a strip of solid black, followed by a strip of white, and then with a tip of black. Make it into the wing, flowing back almost to the end of the tail. For topping, tie in four strands of peacock herl, longer than the tail. (*DD*)

5. BLACK JAGUAR: A black marabou tail of about an inch. A silver mylar body. A generous amount of black marabou for a wing, extending past the tail. Tie in a dozen strands of silver lurex, about two inches long, as a throat hackle. (*Salt*)

6. BLACK SEAL: On a No. 8 long-shank hook, tie in a strand of silver tinsel. Dub in black seal's fur, bringing it up to the eye. Wind on the tinsel, dividing the body into six segments. (*DD*)

7. BLACK WOOL MUDDLER: Cut a dozen strands of black wool half inch long and attach to a No. 8 long-shank hook for the tail. Tie in silver tinsel for rib. Wind the black wool forward toward the eye, followed by the tinsel. Create a muddler head. (*DD*)

8. THE BLEEPER: On a No. 10 hook, attach strands of orange and white feathers, about as long as the body. Tie in a strand of silver wire at the bend. Tie in white marabou at the bend, winding it to the eye. Wind the wire forward, over the marabou, to the eye. Make a throat hackle of orange and white feathers, half as long as the body. Attach the white marabou wing, followed by an orange-dyed feather, and smaller white marabou for topping. (*DD*)

9. BLUE BODY: Tie crow or other black/blue-black feathers on a No. 10 long-shank hook as a tail in generous proportions. Wind the

body of blue metallic Sellotape. Make a generous wing of the black feather. Attach four strands of peacock herl for topping, longer than the tail. Take several turns of some herl to create a not very big head. *(DD)*

10. BRONZE HERL NYMPH: No. 10 long-shank hook. Tie in a luminous yellow wool tail. Follow with bronze peacock herl toward the eye, about three-quarters the way up the hook. Make a collar with that yellow luminous wool. Make a head—not a big one—with the herl, winding the rest of the way toward the eye. Tie in a brown hackle. Tails and collars may be created in other colours, as required. *(SD)*

11. CARDINAL: A red tail feather, fairly generous, about three-quarters of the length of the hook. Follow with gold tinsel for rib. Red tying cotton for body (red wool may also be used instead). Bring the ribbing to the eye. Tie in red hackle, followed by the red feather wing. *(Am)*

12. CHUKAR FLY: If chukar partridge feathers are not available, then French partridge will suffice. Make a tail and body with a long-shank hook of desired size, using the almost yellow, unmarked feathers of the chukar, or if unavailable, a hen pheasant. Make the tail of three feathers, tied flat, one on top of the other. Take three of the multi-coloured striped feathers, placing them flat—one on top of the other, though not evenly—at the eye, and tie down sufficiently far back to make them curve. In other words, the feathers, reaching somewhat past the bend, should make a broad semi-circle around the shank. Attach four strands of peacock herl at the eye, longer than the tail. Make a head of peacock herl wound around the shank at the eye. *(DD)*

13. THE COLLECTOR: Tie a half-inch tail of orange-dyed cock feather onto the bend of a No. 6 long-shank hook. Tie in silver tinsel at the bend, and bring it forward three-quarters the distance to the eye. Tie in a shoulder of red wool. Tie in a dozen strands of orange-dyed cock feathers for a throat hackle, long enough to reach the point of the hook. Tie in generous orange marabou wing, extending well past the tail, followed by a smaller amount of white marabou. Build up a black head, onto which make a white eye, with a red pupil. *(SD)*

14. COON TAIL: Get a racoon tail, not too hard to come by, which is striped black and light tan. Reproduce as a nymph, first tying in at the bend on a No. 10 long-shank hook, the black fur. Follow by the tan in the same way, then a row of black, alternating up to the eye. *(DD)*

15. CORK HEAD: Tie in a strand of copper wire at the bend of a No. 10 long-shank hook. Tie in a piece of silver wire, below the copper wire. Dub on yellow seal's fur, covering up the copper wire, and moving toward the eye, allowing some space below the eye. Tie in a piece of cork here, just below the eye, in two pieces, binding them together in an approximate bullet shape. Carry on with the dub-

bing, over the cork. Bring up the wire, securing the cork, and wind off. *(D D)*

16. COW DUNG: There are at least two other tyings that are English and more than one American tying. The body can be either a dirty orange wool, or green wool, teased out. The hackle is brown. The wings are grey. *(Am)*

17. CRAIG'S NIGHT-TIME: Tie in a tail of red wool. Tie in a strand of silver wire at the back for ribbing. Tie in black wool (or chenille) the length of the hook shank for the body. Wind the silver ribbing to the eye in three turns. A dark-blue feather is fitted over the top, past the tail, topped by a modest bunch of yellow feather strands. *(N Z)*

18. CREAM SEAL: Tie in a strand of silver tinsel, onto the bend of a No. 6 long-shank hook. Dub in cream seal's fur at the bend, bringing it to the eye. Wind the tinsel forward, segmenting the body. Make a throat hackle of half a dozen pheasant-tail feathers, long enough to reach the point. *(D D)*

19. CRUISER: A tail of white feathers, about an inch long, with a stripe of black feathers at the centre. The body is silver chenille tinsel or similar. At the eye, tie in a strip of white goat hair extending past the tail. On top of it, at the eye, tie in an even longer, and more generous, strip of goat hair. *(D D)*

20. CINNAMON NYMPH: Get a hank of 'Goldglow—35821' at your friendly knitting wool department. Tie it in at the bend with green tying thread on a No. 10 long-shank hook, to the eye, winding it off with a head of green thread. Tease out the wool. *(D D)*

21. DARK CAHILL: The tail is approximately 18 strands of pheasant tail or similar, as long as the fly body. Gold wire. The body is grey wool. Wind the wire to the eye. Tie in a brown hackle. The wing is brown, mottled, wood duck or similar. *(Am)*

22. DARK MONTREAL: About 18 claret-dyed feathers for the tail, just over half the length of the fly body. Tie in a gold rib. The body is made of claret floss. Wind the gold ribbing to eye. Attach the claret hackle. Tie in a brown turkey wing, or similar in dark brown. *(Am)*

23. DEER BEARD: Tie in a golden pheasant tippet at the bend of a No. 8 long-shank hook. Wrap the shank with gold foil half-way to the eye. Starting at the centre of the shank, tie in individual peacock herls as a wing, advancing toward the eye. Create a generous throat hackle of natural deer hair, reaching past the barb. *(D D)*

24. DEER HAIR: On a No. 12 hook with a dark brown tying thread, tie in a strand of copper wire at the bend. Wind thread to eye. Wind the wire forward. At the head, attach the deer hair, but making only a few turns, allowing it to flare, but not in fact making a muddler head. Break off and do not trim. The deer hair should extend beyond the fly, and be appropriate in size for the hook *(S D)*

25. DUB HEAD: A body of silver foil over a No. 8 hook. Tie in a generous wing of teal, followed by half a dozen bronze peacock herl feathers. Now, if you have the head of a silver pheasant, there should be a cluster of dark red feathers attached. If these are not

SID'S DISCOVERIES

available, then some other red or scarlet feathers will do. Attach it to either side, at the point where the teal wing has been tied in, as a cheek, so that about a half-inch of it will show. Dub on a generous head of black seal skin. *(DD)*

26. THE GLORIA FLY: On a No. 10 long-shank hook, tie a half dozen white ostrich feathers, none over half an inch, for the tail. Include with them an equal number of the same size strips of silver lurex. With the white tying thread, build up a body, inserting at intervals strips of lurex, starting at the back and working forward. Allow the lurex to extend about half an inch. To anchor them firmly, make a tie over the lurex, fold it over, and a tie over the fold. Continue to do this until a white body, glittering with lurex, has been created. At the eye, as topping, a half dozen strands of white ostrich, and strips of lurex, extending just back of the tail. *(DD)*

27. GOLD BODY PHEASANT: Create a body of gold leaf. Take five of the black-fringed, dark-brown feathers from the chest of a cock pheasant. Tie them flat, one on top of the other, but not evenly, at the eye. Attach four strands of gold lurex at the head for topping, floating past the wing. *(DD)*

28. GREYHOUND NYMPH: Tie in silver wire at back, on No. 8 long-shank hook. Tie in grey-green thread, forming a thin body. Tie in a heron feather at the eye, and wind around shank toward the bend. Wind up the wire toward the eye, forming the rib. Take a few turns of peacock herl to make a head. Tie in about 18 pheasant feathers as topping, three-quarters the length of the shank. Tie in about half dozen pheasant tail feathers for the throat hackle. *(SD)*

29. THE GREEN CATERPILLAR: On a hook you buy, or bend into a semi-circle, wind green wool onto the hook tightly, using a slightly lighter shade of green for tying thread. A third of the way along the body, tie in some legs, four golden pheasant tippets. Advance the next third, and tie in another set of legs. Proceed almost to the eye with the green wool, at which time the third set of legs will be affixed. Make a small head of peacock herl. *(SD)*

30. GREEN TAIL: A green goat hair, extending back almost as far as the extremity of the tail about two inches long, fairly generous. The body is metallic blue, made from Sellotape, cut into strips not much more than an eighth of an inch wide. Wind to eye. Tie in some more of the green goat hair at the eye, extending back to the tail. Tie in a goodly amount of white tail. Follow with an equal thickness of more green goat hair, extending about half the length of the tail. *(Salt)*

31. GREY GHOST: Wind strand of silver wire, meant for ribbing, onto back of hook. Wind silver foil over hook shank to eye. Tie pair of grey hackle cock feathers at eye of hook, top, for wing, flowing well back. Wind silver strand over body and through wing, to eye, in four turns. *(NZ)*

32. GROUSE TAIL MUDDLER: A bushy tail of six grouse feathers on a long-shank hook in a size of your own choosing. Wind the body with gold foil. Tie in half a dozen peacock herl feathers as topping.

Make the muddler head and trim sparingly. *(DD)*

33. HAIRY DOG: Tie a healthy clump of black goat hair or squirrel tail in at the back considerably longer than the hook. Tie silver wire at back for ribbing. Tie in green chenille (or wool) for body, toward eye. Wind silver wire ribbing forward over body, in four turns. Tie in an equally generous amount of black goat hair or squirrel at eye, extending about half the length of the tail. With the same black material make a hackle, extending back well beyond the barb. *(NZ)*

34. HAMILL'S KILLER: Black squirrel tail or goat hair as long as the hook, attached in medium proportions. A small number of orange wisps, tied over the tail, on either side, extending half-way along the tail. Wind the body tightly with yellow wool. Attach two sets, either side, green-dyed partridge feathers, killer fashion (or other green feathers). *(NZ)*

35. HAROLD'S FLY: Tie in a bushy tail of about an inch and a half, of yellow marabou, onto the bend of a No. 6 long-shank hook. Take a piece of white polyfoam, about three-quarters of an inch wide. Roll it around the hook, not too close to the point, making an ample body. Tie black thread a short distance back from the eye, securing it to the shank, and creating a head. Tie a second piece slightly more than midway toward the bend. Many of these foams disintegrate when used in conjunction with varnish. *(SD)*

36. HENRY NICHOLS' FLY: Create a generous tail of orange and red feathers, about three-quarters of an inch long, on a No. 8 long-shank hook. Tie in a strand of silver tinsel. Make a body of orange wool, bringing it to the eye. Wind the tinsel to the eye. Make a hackle of red-dyed cock feather. Tease out the body wool. *(SD)*

37. JOCK SCOTT (plain): This is not an easy fly to make, particularly in a small size. Tie in a gold tag, advancing to the bend. Tie in about a dozen wisps of yellow for a tail. Tie in a black cock feather, making several turns, and a fairly generous butt. Tie in thin gold wire, for ribbing, followed by yellow floss half-way up the shank, then black floss almost to the eye. Wind the gold wire forward over the shank to the eye. The throat hackle, reaching past the barb, is a dozen strands of pheasant tail, or similar. Tie in a pair of wings at the eye of white-tipped turkey, or similar. On either side of the wings, lay in narrow strips of, from top to bottom, blue, red, and yellow. *(Am)*

38. JOE'S HOPPER: It was created as a grasshopper, but appears to be regarded by fish as other things. It started out in the State of Michigan, but made its way West. Tie on a No. 8 hook. The tail is scarlet hackle fibre. The body is yellow chenille or wool, tied in at the back with a few turns of the thread. Leave for a moment, and tie in a brown hackle feather, which will be created as ribbing. Tie the body forward, toward the eye. Follow with the hackle, wound through the body. Leave enough room to attach the wings. These are two matched turkey quill sections, or similar. Leave sufficient room at the eye to tie in two hackles, starting back and working for-

DU BROFF DEPENDABLES

ward. The first is brown, the second, dyed yellow cock. *(Am)*

39. KING OF THE WATER: Tail of grey (mottled) teal or mallard, rather modest. A gold tinsel rib, followed by red tying cotton. Wind the rib to the eye. Tie in the brown cock hackle. Attach the wing, of mallard or teal (mottled). *(Am)*

40. LATIMER FLY: A goodly tail of black marabou, as long as the shank, on a No. 8 hook. Make a body of silver foil. At your option you can tie in a strand of copper wire, running it around the body. Make a throat hackle of marabou, generous, but not over a quarter of an inch long. Attach a generous wing of black marabou. *(DD)*

41. LATIMER SCULPIN: A lot of things are called sculpins, some of them widely different. To try and reduce the confusion we will call this The Latimer Sculpin. It can be tied in any number of ways and sizes, and all of them effective in their own time. It pays to create a substantial variety, since there are times when they will reject one kind with utter contempt, only to take another with great eagerness. Here is the basic tying: A dozen bronze peacock herl feathers as a tail, about one-third the length of the body. Tie in silver tinsel at the bend. Wind the body with white tying thread, followed by the tinsel. Affix the muddler head, allowing a modest amount of deer hair to flow from top and bottom of head. Gold and silver foil bodies are also effective, as well as those in black. *(SD)*

42. LATIMER YELLOW TAIL: On a wide-gaped hook, No. 6 or thereabouts, tie in a modest yellow feather of about half an inch for the tail. Tie about half the body with yellow tying thread, from the bend. From the eye, run black tying thread back over the shank, overlapping the yellow. Tie in a black hackle feather, over the black portion of the shank, bringing it forward to the eye. Tie in the throat hackle, about a dozen strands of teal, reaching almost to the point. Connect the wing, white-tipped, blue-black mallard. In preference or addition, the shank may be tied with silver foil. *(SD)*

43. LITTLE YELLOW KILLER: The Little Yellow Killer can and should be made in an assortment of colours, though yellow has been mighty effective. On a No. 10 hook tie in three strands of peacock herl at the bend, allowing a bit more than a quarter of an inch for a tail. Tie in the gold leaf and wind it the length of the body. Run the herl along the spine of the hook to the eye, and tie it down. Make a generous hackle, using the colour desired. *(SD)*

44. MAGGOT MUDDLER: Bend a hook so that it is hump-backed, or buy one that's already that way, in Size 10. Wind gold tinsel, for the rib, at the bend. Tie in white wool to the eye. Create a muddler head, with some flowing deer hair. *(DD)*

45. MALLARD: The black squirrel tail or goat hair is created as a tail which tapers to a point, starting almost half-way up the hook shank. Wind red wool tightly over it toward the eye. With the streaky black and white (mottled) mallard or teal feathers, tie in two on each side of the hook at the head, killer fashion, formed as wings. *(NZ)*

46. MALLARD SMELT: Tie a thin strip of teal or mallard feathers at back for the tail, almost as long as the hook, followed by a strand of silver wire for ribbing.

Make the body of tightly-wound green floss or cotton. Wind the ribbing over the body in six turns. Tie in a white hackle, extending the length of the body, with the beard reaching the barb. (NZ)

47. MARTIAN: Whisks of yellow on a No. 8 long-shank hook for a tail. A strip of gold tinsel at the bend. At the eye, tie in a white feather, one as stiff as you can find, and wind it around the shank, palmer style, to the bend. Bring up the tinsel ribbing to the eye. Tie in a white wing, one as long as the extremity of the tail. Remember, with this tying, the colour combinations can be infinite. (SD)

48. McGINTY: About a dozen strands of red feathers for the tail, almost as long as the fly body. The body is black and yellow chenille, wound on as if it were a bee. The hackle is brown cock. The wing is white-tipped turkey. (Am)

49. MICKEY FINN: Can be made with buck tail or feathers. If you are using buck tail, don't bother with a tail. If you are using feathers, tie two narrow strips of red and two of the same, of yellow, on a No. 8 hook, as a tail. Wind tinsel on almost to the eye. Tie on a pair of yellow wings. Tie in a red band on each side of the wing, running horizontally, allowing more yellow to show on the top than on the bottom. Make a modest throat hackle of yellow. Use a long-shank No. 8 for a bucktail, No. 6 if you prefer. Tie in the yellow, more on the top than on the bottom, followed by a narrow strip of red, and then more of the yellow. (Am)

50. MINK MUDDLER: If you don't have, or can't locate, a piece of mink, some other similiar fur will have to do. At the bend, for a rib, on a No. 10 long-shank hook, tie in a strip of silver tinsel. Dub the fur onto the body, and wind the tinsel toward the head. Take a thin strip of mink, including the skin to which it is attached, longer than the bend of the hook, and tie down. Create a muddler head with deer hair flowing back from it. (DD)

51. MOORHEN MUDDLER: A slate-black moorhen feather tied in as a tail on a No. 8 long-shank hook. Make a body of silver tinsel. The wing is made from the black and white moorhen feathers, with half a dozen strands of silver lurex tied in with it, all of it extending slightly beyond the tail. Attach a muddler head, fairly well trimmed. (DD)

52. MR HOPKINS' FLY: Tie in a strip of copper wire at the bend of a No. 10 long-shank hook. Tie in bronze peacock herl, winding toward the eye. Dub in yellow seal's fur, as a thorax. Tease it out, bringing it up to the eye. (SD)

53. MR SAM'S NYMPH: No. 14 hook. Wind brown tying thread at the bend. Wind yellow tying thread at the bend. Wind the brown thread continuously along the shank to the eye. Follow with the yellow thread, but in broad spirals, allowing the brown to show through in a proportion equal to the yellow, creating, in other words, a fly striped from bend to eye. Tie in peacock herl, taking it

AMERICAN FLIES
The Lucky 13

2   11   16   21   22

37   39   48   62   67

69   76   85

...and four others

38   49   77   97

NEW ZEALAND FLIES

17   31   33   34

45   46   54   63

70   74   81   91

around the shank at the eye to form a head. *(SD)*

54. MRS SIMPSON: Tie in an ample bunch of black goat hair or squirrel-tail at the point, almost as long as the hook. On either side of the hook, at the point where the tail is fixed, tie in the short green-becoming-brown rump feathers from a cock pheasant. Tie a tight body of yellow wool or floss. At the head, tie in another pair of pheasant feathers, which will overlap about half of the pair at the rear. *(NZ)*

55. OCEAN FURY: A red deer hair, or similar, tail, about 1½ inches long, in a generous quantity. A green metallic body, of Sellotape, or similar, cut into strips of an eighth of an inch. A yellow goat's hair wing, reaching back to the tail's extremity. On top of the yellow, tie in a strip of black goat's hair. Tie in a throat hackle of yellow goat's tail, extending back about two inches. *(Salt)*

56. OLSON FLY: Tie in a dozen tail feathers at the bend, on a No. 8 long-shank hook, for the tail. Tie in a length of copper wire. Tie in white wool, winding about a third up the shank toward the eye. At this point, tie in the red wool, moving toward the eye. Make a generous throat hackle of pheasant-tail feathers. Create a pair of wings from pheasant tail. *(SD)*

57. ORANGE AND BLACK STREAMER MUDDLER: Tie two orange and two black feathers on a No. 8 long-shanked hook for a tail, about three-quarters of an inch long. Entwine strands of orange and black wool, winding them onto the hook evenly, to the head. Take five feathers, considerably longer than the hook, in a mixture of black, and orange-dyed cock feathers, creating a balance between the two colours. Make a muddler head, allowing some of the deer hair to flow backwards. This pattern may be created in other colours, with the muddler head being left off, at the tier's discretion. *(DD)*

58. ORANGE AND RED FLAME: A quarter-inch tail on a No. 10 long-shank hook, of red and orange feathers. Wind the body with gold foil. Attach a set of orange wings to either side, extending past the tail. Attach another set of wings in red, of equal length, over the orange pair. Attach four strands of peacock herl at the eye, almost as long as the wings. *(SD)*

59. ORANGETAIL: A generous amount of orange goat hair, about two inches long. Tie in silver chenille tinsel, if you can get it, for the body. If unobtainable, use mylar. For a feather, tie in goat hair, reaching back as far as the tail, creating, in effect, a continuous strip of orange. Follow that with white on top, reaching back almost as far as the extremities of the tail. *(Salt)*

60. OWEN FLY: Tie in a strand of fairly broad silver tinsel for the rib, at the bend. Tie in black wool, bringing it up about two-thirds the way along the shank. Bring up the tinsel, dividing the body in five sections. Tie in red wool to the eye. Make a throat hackle of a dozen teal feathers, reaching the point. Tie in turkey feather, or similar, for the wing. *(SD)*

61. PALMER CHOMPER: On a No. 10 hook, tie in a longish hank of

pheasant-tail feathers at the bend, meant as a wing case. Tie in a strand of silver wire at the bend. At the eye, tie in a white cock feather, or similar, taking it backward to the bend. Wind the wire over the feather toward the eye. Bring the wing case to the eye and tie down. *(SD)*

62. **PARMACHEENE BELLE:** A strip of red and a strip of white feather for the tail. Swan or similar. The red part can be created with a Magic Marker (make sure it is waterproof). The ribbing is gold wire. The body is yellow wool or floss. Tie the wire over the body to eye. The hackle is strands of red and white. The wing is white, swan or similar, with stripes of red feather somewhat less than half as wide, on either side. *(Am)*

63. **PARSONS' GLORY:** tie in wisps of orange feathers (18-20) at back for tail. Tie in strands of silver wire meant for ribbing at back, to be followed by yellow chenille (or wool) for body. At eye of hook, top, tie in two honey grizzle feathers for wing, touching each other, and extending back past the tail. Wind yellow body material forward, over the wing feathers, to eye. Follow with three turns of silver wire toward eye, segmenting the body in three, approximately even, sections. Tie honey grizzle wisps (about 30) at eye, top of hook, extending back to half the length of the tail. *(NZ)*

64. **PEACOCK EYE FLY:** Tie in a dozen half inch strands of peacock herl onto a No. 8 long-shank hook. Create a body of peacock herl. Tie in six strands of half-inch herl as throat hackle. Now take the eye—the top of the whole peacock feather. Remove the herl on either side, allowing only two strands of the brown part to remain, along with the eye. With the stem still intact, attach it to the top of the hook, flat, winding the thread around the stem, making it curve around the hook. Create a topping of six peacock herl feathers two inches long. Wind herl around the hook at the eye to create a head. Trim the eye at the back, but leaving if sufficiently long to flow well past the head. *(DD)*

65. **PHEASANT MOTH:** On a No. 8 long-shank hook (it can be bigger or smaller, depending upon your own needs and requirements) create a body by entwining red and green wool and winding the result onto the shank to the eye. Take two hen pheasant feathers, those with firm markings, extending well beyond the bend of the hook, tying one on top of the other at the eye, flat, beetle style. It will not matter if the top feather does not lay evenly upon the bottom. Now tie in four strands of bronze peacock herl, longer than the wing. *(DD)*

66. **PHEASANT STREAMER:** On a No. 8 hook, tie down a generous tail of pheasant tail feathers, about half an inch long. Make a wing case at the bend, with additional pheasant tail feathers. Tie in a strand of silver wire at the bend..Wind tail feathers on a shank to the eye. Bring the wire forward to the eye. Tie down the wing case at the eye, bending back the points, which should reach the tail, and tie down at the eye, thus creating a wing. *(DD)*

67. **THE PROFESSOR:** Scarlet tail, approximately a dozen wisps,

5

19

30

55

59

72

82

90

96

at the back. Followed with flat gold tinsel. Wind the shank with yellow floss. Bring up the tinsel. Tie in a brown cock hackle, to be followed by a grey (mottled) teal or duck feather for a wing. *(Am)*

68. POLISH FUR COLLAR: Wind a No. 12 hook with gold leaf most of the way toward the eye. Take two fairly good-size brown hackle feathers and wind on, making in effect a fur collar of somewhat less than half the length of the hook shank. *(SD)*

69. QUILL GORDON: Wisps of grey for the tail. The American dressing uses a peacock eye quill for the body, wound tightly around the shank, but pheasant tail or other fibrous material will do, More grey feathers for the hackle. Wing is brown (mottled) wood duck or similar. *(Am)*

70. RABBIT: Wisps of yellow feathers tied at back, making a thick tail almost as long as the hook. A strand of silver wire for ribbing, tied in at the rear. Wind on red chenille (or wool) for the body. Attach a goodly portion of rabbit pelt at the head, extending back beyond the tail. Wind the wire ribbing through the rabbit fur, around the body, in three turns. *(NZ)*

71. RAINBOW MUDDLER: Tie a silver tinsel body onto a No. 10 long-shank hook. The wing can be made of either appropriately-coloured feathers, buck tail or goat hair. Attach the yellow, followed by the blue, on top of which is the red. Tie in the muddler head. Do not trim excessively. Make the fly bigger or smaller, as the occasion demands. *(SD)*

72. RED COCK: Red-dyed cock feather, about an inch long, with a well-pronounced black centre. A silver mylar body. More red-dyed cock feathers for the wing, with well pronounced black centre. Smaller red-dyed cock feathers for the hackle, extending back as far as the point. For topping, a half-dozen strips of orange lurex about 1½ inches long. *(Salt)*

73. RED RUBBERBAND: Allow the first three-quarters of an inch of a red rubberband to dangle as a tail, at which point attach it to the bend of a No. 10 long-shank hook, with red tying thread. Spiral it around the shank to the eye, binding it down with the tying thread as you proceed toward the eye. Do not stretch the band. *(DD)*

74. RED SETTER: Tie a generous bunch of brown squirrel tail or goat hair in for the tail, about as long as the hook. Tie in orange chenille at back, winding about half-way up hook shank. At this point wind a ginger hackle around the body. Now continue to wind the orange chenille to the eye, at which point another ginger hackle is tied in. *(NZ)*

75. THE ROSELLE MUDDLER: An olive marabou tail, about a quarter of an inch, as a tail, on a No. 8 hook. Tie in a length of silver tinsel. Dub on to the body green seal's fur to the head, followed by the tinsel. Connect the wing at the top with more olive marabou, modestly, reaching back half the length of the tail. Make a reasonably generous muddler head, with some deer hair strands reaching back as topping. *(DD)*

76. ROYAL COACHMAN: A half dozen golden pheasant tippet

feathers for a tail, about as long as the hook. A butt of bronze peacock herl, followed by red tying cotton, three-quarters the way up the shank. Wind another piece of herl around the shank below the eye, where the red cotton has ended. Tie in a brown cock hackle. The wing is white—swan or similar feather will do. White goat hair is sometimes used instead. *(Am)*

77. RUBE WOOD: Let this American come to your rescue. He has come to mine on more than one occasion. On a No. 14 hook, make a tag of red with tying thread. Create a tail, longer than the fly, of four strands of pheasant tail. Make a body of white chenille. Tie in a brown hackle. The wing is strands of mallard, tapering just past the bend of the hook. *(Am)*

78. SALT AND PEPPER: Get some Super Prelude by Sirdar, or its equivalent, BS 984. It is a white bri-nylon with strands of black and lurex running through it. On a No. 10 long-shank hook, make a short tail of green wool. Tie in the 'Prelude', winding it around the shank to the eye. Make a hackle of a green-dyed cock feather. *(DD)*

79. SEAL AND PEACOCK: On a No. 12 hook, tie in a dozen strands of white feathers, about an eighth of an inch long. Wind on a strand of gold wire. Dub on some orange seal's fur, covering about half the shank with it. Tie in about a dozen and a half white feathers at the eye, an eighth of an inch long, fan-shaped, standing up, but leaning slightly forward. With monofilament, tied through the eye, create a V-shaped antenna. Go back to the unfinished body. Tie in bronze peacock herl at the point where the orange seal's fur ended, bringing it to the eye. Wind the gold wire forward to the eye. *(SD)*

80. THE SECRET WEAPON: Tie in black and yellow chenille onto the bend of a No. 10 long-shank hook, winding it to the eye. Wind on a strand of thin gold wire. Attach a black feather—moorhen, rook, Canada goose or other—metuka style, running the copper wire through it and around the body, to the eye. With black cock or similar feather, make a generous throat hackle, reaching almost to the point. *(DD)*

81. SCOTCH POACHER: A tail of black squirrel tail or goat hair, longer than the hook, tied in generously. Tie in the silver ribbing. Make a body of orange chenille. Wind the silver ribbing around the body in six turns. Attach a dark blue feather at the eye, over the top, extending half-way back over the tail. The orange hackle is longish, extending around the fly and reaching back as far as the bend. *(NZ)*

82. SHARK: A mixture of orange and black goat's hair for the tail, bushy, about 1½ inches long. A body of mylar. A sleek orange goat's hair wing, extending the length of the tail. An orange goat's hair throat hackle. *(Salt)*

03. SIKA/SIKA MUDDLER: Wind white tying thread onto a No. 6 hook. Take a piece of the white under-side of a sika deer, or its equivalent, with the skin intact, the hair attached to it. The skin should extend slightly beyond the hook bend. It can be fished this way, or a muddler head can be attached. It is effective both ways, though not necessarily at the same time. *(DD)*

84. SILVER AND GOLD: Make a tail of golden pheasant tippets, about three-quarters of an inch long, attached to a No. 6 long-shank hook. Make a smaller tail half inch long, attached forward of the first tail, also of golden pheasant tippet, followed by a third more modest one, just forward of the second tail. Wind the body with silver tinsel. Tie in black deer hair or similar for a throat hackle, roughly a dozen strands, reaching back as far as the barb. Tie in white swan or goose feather for a wing. Follow, toward the eye, with white marabou. Tie in a short-tippet of golden pheasant for the cheek. Follow with four strands of orange ostrich herl, extending well back beyond the tail. *(SD)*

85. SILVER DOCTOR (plain): (This one is hard, too). Start with silver tinsel for the tag, running in part way up the shank. With red tying thread, tie in half a dozen golden pheasant tippets just forward of the tag. Make a butt with the red thread in about half a dozen turns, covering the tinsel. Wind the tinsel toward the eye. Tie in a generous throat hackle of blue-dyed cock feather. The wing is grey, from a Canada goose, or similar. On either side of the wing, attach narrow strips, from top to bottom, of blue, red, and yellow. *(Am)*

86. SILVER PHEASANT: On a No. 10 long-shank hook, tie in a teal feather tail, about half as long as the body. Wind silver tinsel onto the shank. Tie in teal feathers for a body hackle, long enough to reach the tail. Tie in a wing of silver pheasant tippet, flowing back to the tail extremity. Finish off with four strands of peacock herl for topping, as long as the wing. *(DD)*

87. SILVER STRAND: Tie in a dozen half-inch strands of peacock herl for a tail, on a No. 10 long-shank hook, along with six strands of silver lurex of approximately the same length. Wind a body of silver tinsel. Near the head, make a generous wing of soft, white feathers—swan or other. At the front, tie in a touch of orange. Finish with a topping of six peacock herl strands and six strands of lurex, sweeping back well past the tail. *(DD)*

88. SKATER: This is a hard one, initially, but with some practice becomes rather easy. It can be made in any colours desired, on a fairly small hook. Get two stiff hackle feathers, long enough to create a fly that can run up to two inches in diameter, which is fished dry. Tie in the first hackle at the bend, concave side, up. Run the thread in wide turns along the shank to the eye. Follow by winding the hackle loosely toward the eye, allowing the excess to merely hang loosely. With the fingers push the thread and hackle back toward the bend. Repeat this operation until the hackle has been thus affixed to the hook shank in its entirety. Take the second hackle, and tie it on to the shank, concave side facing back. Repeat the operation with the second hackle, pushing it forward so that the two hackles meet in the centre, creating there an apex. The Skater, skated over the water, will arouse the fish inclined to be aroused. *(SD)*

89. THE SNIPE FLY: Attach a strand of fine silver wire to the bend

of a No. 10 long-shank hook. Tie in two brownish, mottled, long feathers, and wrap them around the hook, stem and all, allowing the backs to form a tail. Bring the wire up the shank, securing the feathers. Take four of the light-coloured feathers, those in which the division, running the length of the feather, is almost yellow, the other part, running in bands of brown; attach two of them to each side of the shank, one on top of the other, allowing them to overlap. With some of the smaller snipe feathers, create a head—one that allows some of the feathers to undulate freely. *(D D)*

90. SURF RIDER: Allow a quarter inch of the silver mylar, created as a body, to unravel. Tie the mylar firmly with black tying thread the length of the body. At the eye, allow about three-quarters of an inch of mylar to unravel. Tie it down firmly. Tie in an orange goat's hair wing, extending past the bend. On top of the orange, tie in a fair amount of black goat's hair, extending slightly beyond the orange. *(Salt)*

91. TAUPO TIGER: Wisps of orange feathers, almost as long as the hook, for the tail. A strand of silver wire for ribbing. Tie in yellow chenille (or wool) body along hook shank. Tie in a pair of badger hackles (with dark centre) at the eye, for a wing, well past the tail. Wind the ribbing through the wing and around the body (metuka fashion) in three turns. Make a head of red tying cotton. *(N Z)*

92. TEAL FUZZY NYMPH: On a No. 10 long-shank hook, tie in a generous teal feather at the bend. Tie in a strand of blue metallic foil at the bend, wind it forward, but leaving spaces on the shank as you wind. Tie it down. Wind the teal feather forward along the space left uncovered. Tie it down at the front *(D D)*

93. TEAL MUDDLER: A variety of sizes is desirable. Tie in a generous tail, approximately half-inch of teal feather. Make a body of gold foil. Tie in a teal wing, extending almost as far back as the tip of the tail. Tie in a generous throat hackle, also of teal. Additionally, similar flies may be profitably created that have strips of orange feathers mixed with the teal wing, as well as white and ostrich herl as topping. Attach the muddler head, retaining some of the flowing deer hair. *(D D)*

94. TONY'S LAST RESORT: Tie in a generous tail of green wool, about half an inch, onto a No. 10 long-shank hook. Tie in a strip of gold tinsel, at the bend. At the eye, tie in black cock hackle, winding it around the shank to the bend, Bring up the tinsel to the eye. *(S D)*

95. WHITE HERL FLY: Create a tail of six half-inch white ostrich herl feathers, attached to a No. 8 hook. Tie in a strip of silver wire. Wind white ostrich herl onto the shank as a body, followed by the silver wire. Tie a dozen white ostrich herl feathers of varying lengths near the eye, as the wing, the longest of which reaches well back past the tail. Take several turns with more white ostrich herl to make a head. *(D D)*

96. WHITE NIGHT: An orange goat hair tail, about an inch long. A red metallic body, made from Sellotape or similar, cut into strips of

approximately an eighth of an inch wide. A green goat's hair throat hackle, fairly generous, approximately three-quarters of an inch long. The wing is white goat's hair, extending well back beyond the tail, in generous amounts. *(Salt)*

97. WOOLLY WORM: On a No. 10 long-shank hook, tie in a quarter inch of triple-strand red wool, at the bend, for a tail. Tie in the black chenille about mid-shank, and wind it back to the bend. Tie in a brown cock feather, concave side forward, at the bend. Wind the chenille forward to the eye. Wind the cock feather over the body to the eye, and tie down. Trim the cock feather. *(Am)*

98. YELLOW BOMBER: On a No. 6 hook attach strands of peacock herl, for the tail, in varying sizes, but none over half an inch. Wind the shank with peacock herl about three-quarters the distance to the eye. Tie in a generous amount of yellow marabou feathers, extending well back past the tail. Now, six strands of peacock herl, as topping, flowing as far as the end of the tail. Make a substantial head by winding on strands of peacock herl. *(SD)*

99. YELLOW CHENILLE MUDDLER: Tie in three strands of yellow chenille for a tail, onto a No. 8 long-shank hook, approximately a half-inch long. Tie in silver tinsel as ribbing. Wind the shank with yellow chenille, toward the eye, followed by the tinsel. Attach the muddler head, allowing a substantial amount of deer hair to flow backwards, along the body. *(DD)*

100. YELLOW SEAL AND BLOOD: Tie in a strand of copper wire at the bend of a No. 10 long-shank hook. Dub yellow seal's fur along the shank, about three-quarters of the distance toward the eye. Dub in red seal's fur to the eye. Make a throat hackle of red or scarlet feathers. *(DD)*

SOME USEFUL SUGGESTIONS

Smoking your own

The fishmonger who smoked that Avington trout that went almost seven pounds could not always cope with other people's fish, and suggested that I smoke my own.

I had the impression that it was pretty difficult. He showed me his smoker. If at the time I had thought it a realistic possibility, I would have asked a lot of pertinent questions. The idea had always appealed to me, but everything I had ever read on the subject led me to believe that it required a high degree of professionalism, profound knowledge, and facilities I did not have and could not create.

But then I ate some of that smoked trout. I knew that I couldn't go on without a regular supply of it. Smoked salmon is (was) one of the things I like best. This was better. In due course I came up with the answers that made it possible to smoke my own and life is even richer now.

Previous reading on the subject said to dig a trench through which the smoke could pass on its way to the fish. My garden is paved over, and very small, so digging a trench is out of the question. You don't need a trench. What you need is something that contains the smoke, something that allows it in, and allows it out. Anything will do, including a metal oil drum. As it happened, I had an old ottoman. The springs were broken and I was sick of looking at the thing. I stripped the fabric, which left me with a box—not too different from a coffin. I stood it up on end. I nailed hardboard onto the front, bottom part, and made a hinged door at the top, to be closed with a bird-cage latch.

I am not suggesting that this is the only way; it is what I did, but I have no doubt that there are many other ways and methods, and your own ingenuity will have a lot to do with what finally emerges. There is scope and there is latitude and no need to slavishly follow any one concept. This is what had put me off all those years; this is what had frightened me. The entire process, though involved, is not complicated.

The idea of the trench (not required here) is to cool down the smoke as it travels along, so that the trout will not cook. That is why the process is known as 'cold' smoking. Heat is the enemy. When that fish emerges it is going to be raw, which is just the way you want it. To avoid the danger of cooking, ignore the saying: Where there's smoke, there's fire. Not necessarily, and not here. There is no need for fire, and hence, no danger of heating.

I put my smoker on legs, and encased the area, in this instance, with fabric, in order to contain the smoke. I can pull up the fabric to gain access to the chamber where the containers holding the sawdust shavings are placed to smoke.

There is a big hole at the bottom of the box that lets in the smoke, with a lot of little holes at the top of the box, that let out the smoke. Inside the smoker, close to the top, I have a bar, on which I hang the fish. This is removable. The bar fits into holes, but you can have a permanent bar, if you prefer. The advantage is that you can attach all your fish to the bar, in your kitchen, if that is where you have been working, then remove it afterwards, with the fish still attached. (There is an ever-present danger of cats, which when there is no smoke about, will be attracted from far and wide.)

With my comparatively small smoker I am able to cope with twenty-four sides simultaneously—that is, twelve fish. The more you can do at one time, the less often you have to do it. But again, these are considerations that will depend upon your own wishes and requirements.

I use two containers for making the smoke—one of them is a biscuit tin, the other is a metal waste basket that I pinched from Nedra. I like to have two, so that I can insure that there is always smoke coming through.

The fuel is sawdust or wood shaving, from a hard-wood tree. Soft woods are resinous—and will injure the flavour of the fish, though some can be mixed in quite safely, which will give your trout an increasingly pinkish hue. The sawdust that you buy in small bags meant for 'hot' smoking is a pretty expensive proposition; a furniture maker will have what you want, since they generally employ hard woods in the manufacture of furniture, but check first. The timber yard probably does not keep its sawdust sorted, though there might be a pile of the hard stuff. You might also have access to the proper kinds of trees in your own garden, in a friend's, or in the countryside—one that has already been cut down—with heaps of sawdust that you need only to scoop up. I gathered up a goodly amount just down the road, courtesy of a hard-wood tree that had been cut earlier.

People sometimes encounter difficulty in keeping the sawdust smoking, without actually building a fire. I use a couple of lumps of charcoal. (I get these started in a tin, with firelighters or other easily-combustible material.)

How long does the process take? Somewhere between four and six hours. It depends on how much smoke you've got coming through. Look at your fish. Do they appear nice and oily? Cut off a piece and taste it. Does it taste right? Then it probably is. Experience will count for a lot, as in everything else. Beware of oversmoking. While you have very wide latitude here, in an effort to insure that it is fully smoked, don't give it too much time in the smoke. It will become soft and mushy. While edible even then, it just won't be as good.

We are of course presuming that you've already got the fish. I keep mine in the freezer until I've saved up twelve good-size ones—and the 'gooder' the size, the better. There really is no minimum size, but the smoking process will reduce your fish to about half its previous weight, so you will be dealing with a lot of bones, and not very much fish. There will be a considerable effort devoted to what is not very much result. I have smoked fish of a pound and a half, but it is better if they are at least two—with 2½ pounds being better, still. There is no upward limit.

Neither is there any need to save up your fish. You can smoke one, almost immediately upon bringing it home. Perhaps you can't wait a moment more than is necessary to start enjoying this delight of delights. Right, then. Start now.

Take a non-metallic container—plastic is fine—one big enough to contain the fish you are preparing to smoke. Cover the bottom with salt. The salt, coarse, if possible, not free-flowing—the idea of the salt is to draw the fluid from the flesh.

When it comes to salting, everybody has his/her own idea about what else should be added. Generally it's brown sugar. I also add white pepper, cloves, crushed bay leaves, garlic powder and onion powder.

Fillet your trout. Don't bother with removal of the bones at this time. It is going to be infinitely easier to do it after your fish is smoked than before.

Lay the fish in your container, skin side down. Cover your fish with a layer of salt, along with whatever else has been mixed into it. Lay the next lot onto it, flesh-side down. Don't over-salt the tail section; being thinner, it requires less salt, and will otherwise wind up saltier than the rest of the fish.

Cover that layer with salt, repeating the process with all the fish that you are intending to smoke. Remember, each layer of fish is placed with flesh resting on flesh.

Trout fillets of up to two pounds a side need six hours of salting in the container. If they are smaller than two pounds, five hours is sufficient. Three-pound fillets need eight hours, and bigger ones, nine. The chances are that you may have a variety of sizes that you wish to smoke. The bigger sides can go in first, at the bottom, in order to allow them more time in the salt.

The container will begin to fill with fluid, drawn from the fish by the salt. When the salting process is completed, wash the fish well with cold water, then soak them in cold, fresh water for five minutes. Drying is not necessary with trout, though it is with salmon.

Put the fish in your smoker, and let the smoke do the rest. Besides sawdust, wood chips and shavings, you can use a log if you can get it to smoke adequately, and without a flame.

When the smoking process is completed, let the fish hang overnight—in the house—to dispel any excess of smoke. They can now be packed in reasonably thick plastic bags, the air drawn out, and adequately sealed, and returned to the freezer, to be consumed as required. It is helpful to keep a record of how many you have put in to the freezer (in a little notebook that tells you at a glance what has been put in) and check it off when it comes out.

As an alternative to plastic bags for storing your smoked trout, you might want to use a double layer of cling film. Seal it with an iron. Lay the iron in a container, heat side up, covered with aluminium foil. Touch the film to the iron for a moment at the points you wish to seal.

As an alternative to salting the fish directly, you can also brine it. Use a pound of salt to a gallon of water. (Add the other spices as desired.) Steep the fillets in this for an hour, remove and allow to dry over night.

So, that's it. It's not difficult and results should be satisfactory right from the start. Eat it and enjoy.

Smoking it hot

There is a lot of confusion about smoking fish. The man with the little box may have wondered why his trout didn't look, taste, or feel like the smoked trout he'd been given some time earlier—that had tasted better than smoked salmon. He need wonder no more. He has 'hot' smoked his fish: in other words—cooked it.

Not to down hot smoked fish. It's delicious. It's another way of preparing your trout, enhancing it with smoky flavour. The other kind of smoking is known as 'cold' and the trout that emerges is raw, which is the way you eat it.

If you are thinking about buying a hot smoker, this is not meant to discourage you; on the contrary, it is one more way of insuring that you take maximum pleasure from the trout you catch and eat. But it is important to be aware of the difference and to know what is involved.

Hot smokers cope with one or two not very large fish. They are put into the box, with some sawdust below. Underneath the box, which is elevated, one places two metal cups; these are filled with methylated spirits and ignited. In about twenty minutes they burn themselves out and the trout, if not too big, will be ready to eat. A thicker fish will require more cooking. It is possible to impart more of a smoky flavour by using only one ignited cup of methylated spirits at the time, and repeating the process several times, remembering to add more sawdust.

The sawdust must come from a hard-wood tree. It is available by the bag and is not cheap. The bag is rather small and it costs in the neighbourhood of a pound. Sawdust, once seen in abundance, is no longer available, it being considered not overly sanitary. The sawdust currently available has been purified and suitable for use in home smoking.

You may have your own source of hard-wood suitable for smoking, which is just fine. But to make any special effort to acquire it would appear to be wasteful, since the amount used is relatively small. For cold smoking, one's own source of hard-wood is highly desirable, since a good deal more is consumed.

What does come high is the methylated spirits. If any amount of trout is to be smoked, one can go through a bottle very quickly. To be able to buy it in bulk quantities will result in substantial savings.

The trout, thus smoked, may be eaten instantly. It may be eaten the next day cold, or reheated. It may be frozen, and eaten at a later date, either hot or cold. Any way you do it, it's going to be nice.

Keeping your fish cool when you are warm

A wasted trout is nothing short of vandalism, even though it may have been involuntary. That fish represents the crown of our success, a magnificent achievement for the fisherman, and the reason for our having come in the first place. It represents a large expenditure in money and effort to create that fish, and to finally get it to where we can catch it. And it represents our aspirations, as well as the goodly amount of money we have had to put out in order to finally land that fish.

It deserves your respect. And it deserves special care to insure that you bring back your fish in first-class condition. It isn't difficult—just a little planning beforehand. As soon as possible, the fish should be degutted.

I keep a cold box in the car, with several ice packs, and put my fish in it as soon as I can, which insures that they will not only keep, but retain their flavour. If it is very warm, I'll keep another, smaller, cold box or bag with me, in the boat or in the bank. And into it I will instantly put any fish I am fortunate enough to catch. A bag and a few ice packs will not add significantly to the fisherman's burden.

Plastic bags are not too satisfactory, except for the very shortest of intervals and for transport. Far better is a straw bag, which when dipped in the water, will, with any kind of breeze blowing on it, create its own refrigeration. The bag, dipped as it starts to dry, should be kept in the shade, with grass between the fish. I find a bag made of jute to be equally satisfactory. It has the advantage of being flexible and can be washed more readily.

If it is a trip of some duration, there are other problems to consider. Those ice packs will not remain frozen for twenty-four hours, despite the claim made for them, particularly if the weather is very warm. However, they serve their purpose, and if you have enough of them, with access to a freezer for the night, you can alternate. But more effective are blocks of ice. Freeze one or more in a gallon-size plastic ice-cream container and put it (or them), in your cold box. During a particularly hot period the ice lasted for three days and kept the contents cool. The box was shaded, which contributed substantially to the longevity of the ice. In the boot of the car it would not have lasted as long.

Carry extra containers so that when the ice is melting in your box, another gallon or so is being frozen. The containers need not be gallon-size if this is not convenient or expedient; those who provide freezer space for you on a temporary basis might not have the room for large-size containers, so it is better to be prepared with some smaller ones. The inside of your cold box should be covered at the top with a sheet of polyfoam or something similar, which provides further insulation.

If where you happen to be fishing, they have freezer facilities, that can be convenient. But it is important not to let the fish defrost during the journey home. Put the fish in your cold box, along with the ice packs or containers of ice, which should be good for six to eight hours, depending upon the weather. If you don't have a cold box with ice, wrap the fish in thick layers of newspaper which will provide insulation and keep the cold in. If the fish should defrost before you get them home, cook them, then put them in the freezer. By virtue of having cooked them, you have altered the chemical composition of the fish and they may now be refrozen with complete safety.

For freezing, make sure your fish are dry both outside and inside. Freeze in a thick plastic bag, with the air removed, or in a double layer of cling wrap. The fish should never be exposed to freezing without adequate protection, which otherwise could cause freezer burn, and hurt the flavour of the fish.

Proper handling creates its own reward—when we eat our catch. Naturally we want it to taste as nice as was intended. It was indeed worth catching; the greatest compliment that we can pay is that it is worth eating.

If you want to keep it — salt it

You may be in some remote area where there are no freezing facilities available. You've got an abundance of fish, which you are eager to keep, to bring home and eat over an extended period. Then salt them.

Clean and scale your fish. Fillet and dry. To the salt (not free-flowing) you can add such spices as chopped dill, celery salt, whole peppercorns, and if you like, brown (soft) sugar.

You can use a plastic pail, a wooden bucket or earthenware crock. Cover the bottom with a layer of your salt mixture, put in the fish, flesh-side down. Cover with more salt and add another layer of fish, also flesh-side down, until completed. Cover the container firmly. Keep it in a cool, dark place for seven to ten days.

If more fish becomes available each day, use a separate smaller container, or otherwise note the addition of these new fish.

Upon returning home, remove the fish from the container, and store in the refrigerator, where it will keep up to six months in a temperature of 40°. Alternatively, it can be frozen.

For use, in quantities required, run cold water on the fish. Cover it with cold water, and let it stand over night. Rinse again and dry it. Cook it like you would if you had just caught it.

If circumstances are such, you can salt your fish as outlined above, but retaining it in the salt solution for one to three days. This shorter process does not preserve it, and your trout should be eaten soon after you have removed it from its container, or frozen until required.

Should you want to store your fish for an extended period, without either a freezer or refrigerator, follow the ten-day process as above. Then take the fish out of the bucket and dispose of the salt solution in which they have been kept. In another container, make a new brine solution by first adding boiled water, to be followed by a goodly measure of salt. When the salt stops dissolving in the water, you have sufficient salt.

Scrape down your trout, getting rid of any clinging salt. Put all your fish back in the bucket. Pour the now cooled brine over it completely. Cover the bucket with butter muslin, and store for two weeks in a cool, dry place.

Your trout is now preserved. Remove it from the bucket and store it in a cool place. It's good for six months. You can keep it in the refrigerator, but do not freeze it under any circumstances.

Fish stored out of a refrigerator will keep for a shorter period during the warmer months than during the colder period, so it is important to be cognizant of this in planning.

Prepare for cooking in the same manner as above.

Those dark fish

If you take some of those dark fish, don't despair. Don't give them away, and certainly don't throw them away. The eating quality of the very dark ones is, as we know, not first class. But that does not mean that we can't turn them into a culinary delight.

Fish cakes! That's right. That's what does it. They're delicious. Those dark fish need never again be a liability. If you have the facilities, you might want to store them in your freezer until there is a sufficient number to make up a large quantity of fish cakes at one go. They can then be returned to the freezer, to be eaten as required, hot or cold. It's a real treat. And should you have the misfortune to run out of dark fish, one could understand the need to employ trout (or other fish) which is in perfect condition. Now we need never to waste our precious fish again. Here is how to do it:

Fish Cakes
Cooked, flaked fish
Salt and pepper to taste
Sage or mixed herbs as desired
Bread or cracker crumbs
For every two cups of cooked, flaked fish, use *one egg* and *half cup minced onion* (more or less onion, as desired)
Put fish in boiling water for ten minutes. Flake fish.
Beat eggs. Mix fish, seasoning, onions, eggs together. Add enough crumbs to bind into fish cakes. Wet hands; form into smooth cakes or balls of required size.
BOIL: Put into boiling water and boil gently for twenty minutes. Carefully remove from water.
FRY: Roll in crumbs. Fry in butter, margarine or oil until brown on both sides.
BAKE: Bake in medium oven for half an hour.

Obtaining fly-tying materials

The fox that got the duck will leave the feathers. You may just happen to come upon them in the course of moving around the lake. You've got scissors with you, so just cut off the feathers from the somewhat unpleasant remains and put them in your fishing bag. Better if you have prepared in advance with a couple of plastic bags carried in a convenient pocket for anything you might encounter along the way that will be useful, and free.

I've always got my Swiss Army knife with me, the one with the scissors, because life is filled with opportunities for obtaining fly-tying material, both inside and outside. A dead bird—if it hasn't been dead too long—will probably have useful feathers. Skin it out (see the section on preserving skins and capes). Almost anything you find will have an application in the creation of flies. If nothing comes immediately to mind in the world of existing flies, think about it for a bit, and invent something new.

Driving along in Georgia, USA, I encountered a dead racoon on the side of the road. It had probably been hit by a car, and didn't appear to be long dead. I really wanted that tail; it had to make some very useful flies. I cut it off and put it in the plastic bag I just happened to have with me. Nedra thought me a bit ghoulish, but she was really lucky that I didn't skin out the whole 'coon—and I would have done, had we not been in such a hurry.

Christmas brings its own special joy to fly fishermen. Christmas tree decorations are often a source of great reward—your own, as well as other people's. Help yourself to any items you think might be useful, nobody will miss them, and long after Christmas is past, you will remember it, along with the generosity of your friends—as a trout strikes that fly made with a bit of angel fluff.

If you are a shooting man, you will have an endless supply of fur and feathers. If you aren't, you may know someone who is. And if you don't, you can often pick up a good buy at a butcher shop that also deals in game. There is grouse, duck, partridge, pheasant, woodcock, hare and rabbit. Not only do you get the fur and/or feathers, you also get to eat the game.

And if you can get hold of a deer skin, you'll be in muddlers for life.

If you should encounter a pigeon—dead or alive—ignore it. Pigeon feathers are unsuitable for tying flies. They get soggy. But the chances are that on any water you are near, there are swans, who in the course of grooming themselves, will have shed many a feather—useful feathers in all shapes and sizes and textures, including lovely marabous. Use them as they are, or colour them with Magic Marker pens, available in a multitude of colours (make sure the Magic Marker ink is waterproof).

Bird zoos can also be a good source, and sometimes a friendly attendant will offer special help. Try to get hold of peacock feathers—those that are shed from the chest and sides. I have never seen these for sale—it's the tail feathers that can be bought. But these little fan-like blue-green beauties are about an inch wide, and can at times be extremely effective. On one occasion, when almost no fish were being taken from a lake being fished by a multitude of hopefuls, those peacock feathers really paid off.

A visit to the farm must also produce rich rewards—cock feathers, bits of raw wool shed by sheep. And remember plastic bags; they come in several colours and are free. Pan scrapers make excellent ribbing; one goes a long way, though the silver scrapers do not appear to be available here. I had to go to Sweden to find mine. It is hoped that the manufacturers of pan scrapers will grasp the need for the silver variety. Metallic Sellotape comes in red, green, blue, silver and gold, is strong and easy to work with. As body material it is also extremely effective, in all of its colours. You cut it to the desired width and wind it on to the hook shank.

Rubber gloves that have sprung a leak and are about to be thrown away—shouldn't. Cut them up and use them for those rubber-body flies. For wool try the knitting section of any department store. No need to feel self-conscious. The variety available will be a source of great pleasure, as well as inspiration. Don't be afraid to seek help from the usually pleasant ladies who serve in such departments. Tell them what you want it for; they will be amazingly helpful and sympathetic. They will regard you with complete seriousness, aware that what you are doing requires a high degree of craftsmanship—on no less a par than those who come for help with their knitting problems.

Here you can also buy tying cotton—in larger quantities, and at prices considerably less than when bought in tiny amounts. Lurex may also be available here, in gold and silver, excellent material for topping. If you should encounter difficulty in finding it, try an Indian shop, one frequented by the Indian ladies who employ lurex on the saris they wear.

The electric shop is excellent for spools of copper wire, good for winding around hook shanks in order to make them sink faster and deeper. Flex that no longer has an application will have usable wire inside, to tie under, or over, fly bodies. Buy varnish in large quantities, and rubberbands, particularly red ones, also have their use when wound around a hook shank.

If the quantities are greater than can be used in the foreseeable future, share them out with fellow fly tiers who will no doubt have items they will want to share with you.

To the list of suggestions here, you will no doubt be able to add many of your own.

Making things with sheepskin offcuts

For seventy-five pence I got a big bag of sheepskin offcuts, which have been put to good use. The FLY PATCH, for example, easy to make and an item I have found extremely useful. Since you fit it over your head, it isn't necessary to punch holes in wax coats in order to attach it.

The patch can be of any dimension you find convenient. Mine is 4 × 5 inches. A heavy duty kilt pin is installed at the top. A leather boot lace, of about a yard, is tied to either end of it. That's it—simplicity itself. I find it useful even when fishing from a boat—I lay it down on the seat and anchor my flies to it after they have been removed from the leader. Exposed to the air, they dry more quickly.

The FLY WALLET is also simple to make. If you have a good-size offcut, fold it in half—approximately five inches by ten—but it can be bigger or smaller, depending upon your own requirements.

Sew some press studs at either corner; velcro would also serve, or even hooks and eyes. This is for closing it when not in use.

Now take the other boot lace and tie it to either corner, which, like the fly patch, you slip over your head for use.

Should you not have a sufficiently large offcut for a one-piece wallet, take two smaller pieces and cut them to equal size and sew them together. Your fly wallet is now completed, available for immediate use.

For fleecy INNER SOLES, the offcuts need to be as big as your feet. If you already have inner soles, lay them down on top of the sueded side of the sheepskin and trace them, then cut out. They are bound to fit. If you don't have inner soles, stand on a piece of cardboard, with your foot firmly on it, and draw your foot, though it is better if somebody else draws it for you.

Cut out the drawing of your foot, put it on the sueded side of the sheepskin and trace. For the other foot, turn over the cardboard, and trace it onto another piece of sheepskin. Cut them out and you now have genuine fleecy inner soles.

Save that anchor

Ken Sinfoil, who was the Head Bailiff at Weir Wood, and has since taken over at Bewl Bridge, told me about anchors, the result, I suppose, of having seen so many lost. Often an anchor attaches itself to something on the bottom and can't be brought up. Ken has devised a method of saving your anchor. He explained it to me.

At Bewl Bridge the explanation, complete with drawing, was put up as a large sign board, and will, probably, one day, save your anchor.

Fix the anchor chain to the bottom of the anchor, adding a shackle, if necessary.

Run the chain along the shank to the shackle at the top. Connect the chain to the top shackle with a piece of not-too-strong string. Should the anchor get stuck on the bottom, the application of additional pressure on the anchor line will break the string. This will permit the anchor to be pulled free, from the opposite direction.

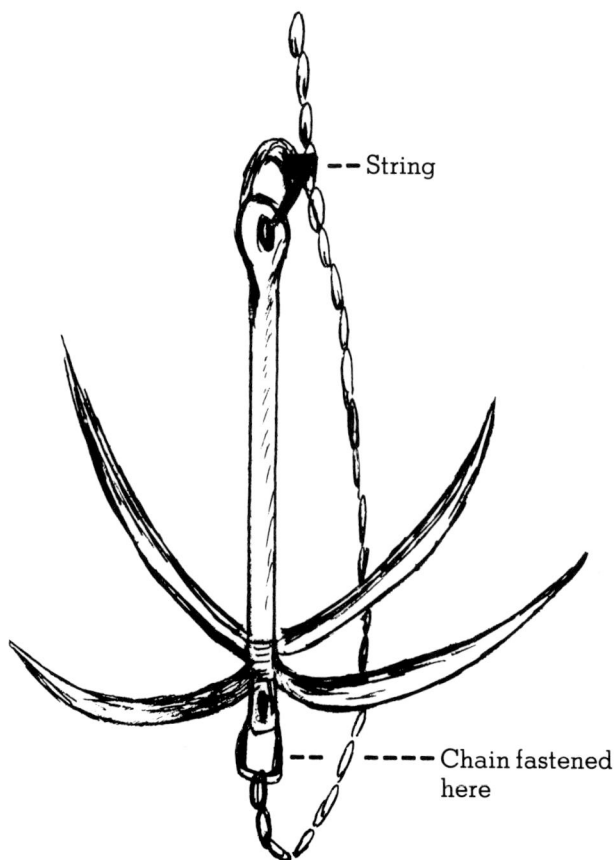

- - String

- - - - - Chain fastened here

It leaks

'It rained all day, and my coat leaked. I got soaked.' This is a complaint frequently heard by wearers of waxed coats. Yet, a waxed coat is about as good protection as you can get. The wax, applied at the factory, will, in due course come off. Particularly vulnerable are the creases, the area where there is any amount of rubbing or abrasion. This can be caused from such things as rowing a boat—arms rub against the sides of the coat—or even from the strap of a fishing bag carried over the shoulder.

The only solution is to rewax the coat. It's no great problem. Buy a tin of wax, usually where they sell waxed coats. It has been suggested that the coat be put in the oven, and then to apply the wax. I find it difficult to believe that anyone making such a suggestion has in fact ever waxed a wax coat in this manner. The impracticality of it appals me.

However, a much easier method is to buy a paint brush, if you don't already have one, when you buy your can of wax. Hang the coat up where there is access to as much of it as possible, where nothing else touches it, and where nothing below it could suffer an injury. If there is any question, put some newspaper down on the floor under it.

Take the lid off the tin of wax. Put the tin on the gas ring or electric plate of your cooker and heat. The wax, white and solid when cold, will turn thin and watery-coloured when heated. It is now ready to apply.

Take that paint brush, dip it into the wax, and paint the wax onto your coat thoroughly. Paint the whole of it, paying special attention to the seams, often the place where leakage occurs.

If you can maintain a low heat under the can, then leave it on the stove. If you are unable to do so, or if the source of heat is somewhat removed from the coat, it is best to work with the wax close to the coat. In time the wax in the can will cool and harden, making it necessary to reheat it.

Allow the coat to hang overnight, where nothing is touching it, and where there is a good circulation of air. When the wax cools, it will harden, leaving white patches. Most will disappear when thoroughly dry. Those that remain can be rubbed in with your finger.

Your wax coat is now renovated, the leaks sealed. How long it lasts depends upon the kind of treatment it gets. With this method you can apply the wax selectively, to specific areas that require it, rather than doing the whole coat over again. But it is better to do a whole wax job from time to time rather than to take a chance on getting soaked.

Getting the hook out when the barb is in

I was telling Alec Pearlman, noted photographer and fly fisherman, how I had got a fly lodged behind my ear, barb firmly implanted in my scalp. It needed an anaesthetic and a doctor to remove it. Alec said it was too bad he wasn't there—he could have removed it without any of the fuss. He had learned the technique from Jeremy Bisley, former chief over at Black Swan. Not only had he learned it, Alec informed me, but had practised it—on a doctor, with another doctor looking on. Too bad he wasn't there when the barb of that hook penetrated my flesh.

Alec says this method works very well, is quick, and virtually without pain.

Loop a piece of string, leader, or even a shoe lace around the bend of the hook.

Keep the string flat against the skin.

Press the eye of the hook against the skin and hold it there.

With the end of the string held firmly—jerk it hard—and fast. The quickness with which it is done makes it a virtually painless operation.

Make sure that the string is long enough to allow you enough leverage for a quick and powerful jerk. And remember that you must hold the eye of the hook flat against the skin with the other hand as you jerk.

The little blood that flows will clean the wound. Dab with antiseptic cream and cover with a plaster. (The fisherman should carry these things in his bag as a matter of course.)

With the hook removed, the fisherman can then return to his fishing. Hopefully he has been inoculated against tetanus—a precaution every fisherman should take. If it hasn't been done previously, it should be done as soon as possible.

Preparing your feather/fur capes

You have acquired fur or feathers, still attached to its original owner, for which it is has no further need. You have killed it yourself, obtained it from a friend who has, bought it at the game dealers, or even found it.

Now the next step is to separate the fur/feathers from the body. It is not a particularly hard job, and practice will make you better at it. The chances are, the bird or animal, having been shot, may not now have an outer layer that is in perfect shape. You are not a taxidermist, so don't worry too much if it should be less than perfect. Just do the best you can. The point here is to salvage as much of that skin, with whatever is attached, as you possibly can.

A trimming knife is a good thing to use, one of those devices with a sharp, thin blade, often employed for intricate work. If it is a bird, get rid of its head and legs by cutting or chopping, depending upon what is available to you. Break the wing bones and remove the wings. Don't throw them away. Cut a slit above the vent, about half-way up, and peel the skin, working it with your fingers. Pull the skin over the legs and wing bones, cutting the rest of the way up.

You now have a skin. Pin it to a board, feather side down, stretching it slightly. You can use a mixture of borax and alum in equal parts, sprinkled on and rubbed in. You can also use salt, which is cheaper, but make sure it is not the free-running kind. In about a week your skin is ready (alum/borax mixture is quicker) preserved with the feathers available for use.

With the wings, slit the area containing the bone and pull it out. Sprinkle with salt or alum/borax. Wildfowl, with its abundance of fat, will need scraping. With a rabbit or hare, or other animal, follow the same procedure as for birds. If the skin is particularly bloody or dirty, rinse it off in warmish salt water.

With hare's ears, scalp the hare around the ears. Remove the unnecessary bits, pin out the ears and salt it down, or use alum/borax.

It comes easier with practice, and this, like all the other things connected with fly fishing, will be a source of pleasure. It is lovely to have the entire cape spread out before you, say of a cock pheasant, and to select the feathers from it that you want to use.

You don't have to be cold

It's spring, generally, when the trout season opens, at least according to the calendar. But often enough spring weather isn't around the corner, and might be a long ways off. In reality it is still winter, with the cold lingering well into the season. If you are shivering, there is little by way of consolation to tell yourself that warmer weather is just around the corner. What about now? The cold can ruin your day, spoil those precious hours of which we have so few, and possibly land you in bed with problems that could be serious.

You don't have to shiver, and you don't have to suffer. You can laugh at the cold, the sleet, the hail, the rain—all the things that are so often a part of that early fishing. You can go on fishing, impervious to what Mother Nature has sent along to try you, sorry for those who are not better prepared.

Are you wearing a hat? Up to 50% of the body's total heat can be lost through the head if it's uncovered. Hats with ear flaps will also protect the ears. You need layers of clothing, things that can be easily peeled off should it grow warmer mid-day, and put back on with ease toward evening as it grows colder. Fly fishing, though strenuous, as we all know, just doesn't generate sufficient heat to keep us warm. Thermal underwear, both tops and bottoms, is a good place to start. I myself prefer to put it over normal underwear. Then a nice, thick, heavy pure wool shirt. And then a down waistcoat. It will ensure that the cold won't get to you, and keep you smiling while others are shivering. It is without a doubt one of the great joys of life—and never mind the cost. It's worth it. But make sure it's down, if you can, though the synthetic-filled models will also contribute substantially to your comfort.

Over the down waistcoat goes a heavy wool sweater. And over that goes the lined, waxed coat. It has a hood, which will be up, and which will keep the wind off. The instant the hood goes up, you feel the difference.

I'm wearing gloves, made of plastic outside, and nicely-lined inside. Created for fishermen, part of the thumb and index fingers are missing on both hands. This allows you to retrieve the line and to change flies without removing the gloves. Functioning is slightly restricted and casting a tiny bit clumsy, but not sufficiently so to justify freezing hands.

Wear a muffler, made of wool, thick and heavy. If your neck is warm, your head and your feet, the rest of you will be, too. Wear waxed over-trousers for further protection.

Feet are a problem, greatly exacerbated if one is fishing from a boat. They—feet—just aren't given the opportunity for movement that would encourage circulation, and hence, adequate warmth. To make things worse, you are probably wearing rubber boots; these are not very good at contributing to warm feet, which may be immersed in snow and/or in almost-freezing water. Wear two pairs, even three, if necessary, of heavy wool stockings. Keep a thermos jug handy, containing a warm drink.

Life will be different on those early fishing trips. It's not a question of endurance, but of creating comfort, in what is basically an uncomfortable situation. You are there to try and catch fish, but if the weather forces you to desist, you are beaten early, and what otherwise would have been pleasure, is now the profoundest pain.

Incidentally, if one sweater over your down waistcoat is not sufficient, then wear two. Outer garments that can be buttoned or zipped are more desirable than those that need to be pulled over the head for removal.

Dressed this way, I have been able to remain outside indefinitely, aware of the cold only because my fellow fishermen complain so bitterly about it. I'm there, where the fish are, dropping my fly onto that cold water.

FLY FISH THE SEA

Fly fishing in the sea has some obvious advantages, like, for example, eliminating the need to buy a day ticket or licence, or to be governed by a bag limit. Neither are there starting or finishing restrictions. The fish are generally good fighters and good to eat. They will take a fly with alacrity—sometimes—and are not usually as selective as trout; and the sea offers an infinite variety of fish. In the United States they even fish for sharks with fly and fly rod.

Fly fishing in the sea can offer a happy compromise when families clamour for a holiday on the beach. Readily agree, which might arouse suspicion, and go to work planning your equipment. It's going to be different from what is normally used, particularly when it comes to flies, though not necessarily all that different.

The flies are going to be bigger, and heavier, and the wind may be a factor somewhat greater than is the case on still water. Consequently you want a line that can cope with the fly, and a rod that can handle them both. The fish aren't stocked, so they are not necessarily there just because you are. Many are migratory and move with the seasons. So it is essential to know what fish, if any, will be present in the area you intend to fish during the period you are there. The weekly fishing newspapers that deal with sea angling will have much of the pertinent up-to-date information.

Another factor that we do not ordinarily consider is the tide. Fish feed on the incoming tide, and when it recedes, so do they. The tides are in and out twice during a twenty-four hour period, with the time varying at each location, as well as with the passage of each day. Tide tables are available for each area around the British Isles where it is possible to fish, and any time spent with these will not be wasted.

Another thing about tides—they come in fast. Your high and dry rock perch is, with a speed that is both amazing and frightening, submerged beneath the water, with the waves licking at your boot tops. So be alert to this, always cognizant of the route that will permit you to take refuge from the encroaching sea. The hour between the tide coming in and going out is known as the slack tide, and for just a little while there is no movement. This may well be the most productive time of all for fishing. Try, if possible, to arrange to be on the water at slack tide. There are, however, fish that remain amongst the rocks, more or less oblivious to the tides, and may provide a bit of sport.

The warm Sunday at Salcombe in Devon was not exactly the most propitious time—or place—to be fly fishing in the sea. The tide was out; the beach was crowded—with bathers and boaters, manning all sorts of crafts, of every size and description. A woman, commanding a push-chair, pushed her child through the surf. I made my way out onto the rocks, which jutted out a considerable distance. In a little while two small boys in a rubber dinghy made a landing on my rocks, mooring their boat more or less permanently and exploring around and about.

Just off the rocks, an anchored launch was haven to a group of people receiving instructions in the art of skin diving. In due course, equipped with their newly-acquired knowledge, dressed in their wet-suits, they immersed themselves in the sea. I very much hoped that my catch would not consist of one or more skin divers, and that my line would pass either over or under them.

Changing rocks, I moved to some that were considerably less inviting (for other people) and considerably less accessible. Here I let my orange sea fly display itself to any fish that may have remained indifferent to the tide. It was quiet for a time. I retrieved with varying rates of speed, and depths, and began to wonder if this was not the wrong fly for this moment in time. I ended the retrieve and took the fly from the water. At that instant a fish—a rock fish that I could not identify—jumped completely out of the water in pursuit of that fly. It was not a big fish—about half a pound—but it certainly was an enthusiastic one.

At Wembury, in Devon, there was considerably more space. Here I encountered a Scot who was surprised to see a fly rod in this alien environment. It was possible, he said, to take bass closer to the estuary, or even sea trout and salmon that were waiting for the river to come right so that they could move up it. Also, there were often mackerel in abundance.

The rocks went out a long way, and so did I. They weren't nice rocks, but sharp up-and-down slabs, like roof tops, with caverns in between that would soon fill up with water, as the tide surged forward. To assist me, I used a walking stick—either it or a wading staff are essential items if one is to fish from the rocks. It is also important to be highly mobile, to be able to retreat, or to even go forward, unencumbered—or as little encumbered as possible.

I cast down into the surf. The wind howled a bit. In a little while I wasn't casting down any more. The surf had come up and now it was licking my boots. A couple of casts more and it covered most of them. It was obviously time to go, to find a less submerged place.

As I retreated, I came upon a peninsula that looked as if it might give me sanctuary, at least for a time. I cast from it, conscious of the short span of time allotted to me here. But not sufficiently so. My peninsula was on an island. This, incidentally, is one of the disadvantages of sea fishing.

I was completely surrounded by water. When a wave broke on the rocks, I was considerably more surrounded. And with the tide coming in at this alarming rate, there was going to be even more water separating me from the rocks that would ultimately lead me to shore.

It was: Jump now—or in a minute things were going to be even worse. I jumped. Without that walking stick I don't think I could have made it, without at least some cut hands—and I hate to think what else. As I moved inland I became aware of a person some distance along, on the rocks adjacent to the shore. It seemed to me that sheer cliffs grew up behind him. Would the tide come in as far as he was? Apparently. Did he know? I hoped so.

Nearing the shore I saw what looked like two young children. One of them was waving to me and calling. Were they in trouble? I didn't feel like rescuing anyone. It was cold, and drizzly and windy, and those rocks were sharp. But no, they didn't need help. As I got closer I saw that they were not in trouble. They approached me. The girl was about eleven, the boy a year or so younger. They thought at first that I was their father. He was the man on the rocks. They were confident that he wouldn't be trapped by the advancing sea. From Manchester, this was their second year here, camping nearby. Last year the father had fished every day for two solid weeks—and hadn't caught anything. That was certainly encouraging.

Now we were safely on the beach. Nedra came by then. 'Don't,' she said to the little girl, 'ever marry a fisherman.'

'I won't,' she assured Nedra.

Later, fishing in the estuary, I got into some mackerel that took my flies readily.

The sea offers many opportunities for the fly fisherman.

An English fly falls in the California desert

On first glance England and Southern California would appear to be very different from each other. But looking more closely, at least from a fishing point of view, you soon become aware of the similarity. Since Southern California has little by way of its own water, it needed to create reservoirs to store what was brought in, as well as to capture the relatively small, and varying, amount that Nature provided during the winter season. So lakes were created, and stocked with trout, a procedure we understand very well from our English experience. But the net results between the two places differ enormously, with England coming out way ahead, despite the vastly superior resources available in Southern California.

The California Department of Fish and Game stocks sixty-eight bodies of water in the seven southern counties, with 2,116,000 'catchable-size' trout. This is done the year round, except in waters that become too warm in summer to sustain trout life; there is, generally, no closed season. These reservoirs are owned or controlled by the various water districts or other public agencies, similar to our own in England. They make no payment for the stocked trout, provided their facilities are open to the public, without special charges for fishing. The costs of such stocking, as well as all other expenses incurred by The Department of Fish and Game, are borne mostly from the sale of fishing licences, purchased by 2,136,500 fishermen state wide, above the age of sixteen (below that age they are exempt). The basic licence costs about £2.40, add another £1.20 for fishing inland waters (as opposed to the salt water), and another £1.80 for a trout stamp—a total of £5.40 for a year's fishing anywhere in the State of California.

Some of these waters may, in addition to Department stocking, stock with trout from private sources, for which they pay. In addition there are privately-owned reservoirs, not stocked from public funds, which make their own arrangements for the supply of trout.

Nedra and I started out what was a visit home to Southern California with a trip to Lake Castaic, a 2600 acre reservoir, forty-five miles from the heart of Los Angeles, operated by the County of Los Angeles, Department of Parks and Recreation. The water here comes down from the northern part of the state, where, until the most recent drought, they had a surplus, through a 337-mile aqueduct. A boat costs £6.00 for four hours' hire, complete with motor; or you can bring your own, which costs 90 pence for a daily permit to launch it, £6.00 annually. During the summer and at weekends they charge 90 pence for car parking.

This was January and fairly warm. The rains had not come; the grass around the reservoir was parched brown. At one point during our stay the thermometer reached ninety degrees. But the nights are cold—desert cold—the kind of cold that seems to penetrate any amount of clothing.

I unlimbered my fly rod—and I was the only one who did so. All the rest used spinning gear or bait-casting equipment, usually still-fishing with whatever they thought might be most effective. I couldn't actually bring myself to put on anything other than a fly, though there wasn't any law that said I couldn't.

Other fishermen looked on with interest—they knew about fly fishing, admired it, respected it, but would probably never try it. There is a certain mystique about it, an awareness that one must *learn* to do it.

Now I dropped my flies into this desert lake. In addition to trout, there are bluegills, crappies, and bass, all of which can be caught on flies—and catfish (the family *ictaluridae*) some of whose members will take a fly. Primarily a warm-water fish, 'cats' are popular in the American South. They are scaleless, with whiskers like that of a cat (hence their name) and are considered a great table delicacy.

For trout there is a limit of five, the same for black bass; ten for catfish, but none for crappy or sunfish. These are limits set statewide by the Department of Fish and Game, but vary according to local conditions.

Late in the afternoon a large tank-lorry backed up to the water's edge. The hatches were opened and thirteen-thousand trout poured out in a steady stream that transferred them to their new home in a few minutes. As if overcome with the joy of so much room they raced up and back, parallel with the dam, about fifty feet out, spurning my flies, as well as all the other delicacies that were offered to them. They were not big fish—about four to the pound. So this was what they meant by 'catchable size.' Ours, I thought, remembering our English lakes, are bigger.

The policy is to stock with a lot of fish often. However, few of these fish seem to grow into anything more, and relatively few appear to be caught. Consequently, the programme has come under a lot of criticism, which, it would seem to me, is justified.

We next went to Lake Sherwood, a privately-owned reservoir north-west of Los Angeles. It was January 15th, and, as it turned out, opening day—never my favourite time to be fishing. There were three hundred people on the lake, which it could easily absorb without overcrowding, though most of them gathered together around a small pool into which the trout had been stocked. The majority of trout were small, half a pound or less, but with the occasional bigger one to add interest. The favourite bait was cheese; however, knowledgeable fishermen select Velveeta—a brown processed cheese resembling a pellet.

I stuck to my fly rod, and on a Royal Coachman made my best catch—the straw hat of a man fishing near me. It had blown off when a sudden gust of wind came down through the canyon. On the second cast I hooked it firmly and returned it to its owner, who was greatly impressed by my skill as a fisherman. Later in the day I spotted a man with a fly rod, which he used with obvious trepidation. Joining him, in a desire not to be such a uniquely exotic species, I discovered that the fly rod was an instrument new to his touch; he had bought rod, reel, line—and fly—for three dollars at a garage sale (held by private individuals, in their garage or back garden to dispose of no-longer-wanted objects, often prior to moving house).

The cost of fishing here is £1.80 a day for adults, 60 pence for children under twelve, with all fish caught belonging to the fishermen. Species and bag limits are similar to those of Lake Castaic. A state fishing licence is required, and armed game wardens make sure that everybody who fishes is in possession of one. A boat can be hired for £3.60 a day, and you can use your own motor, of five horse-power or less. The catfish record here stands at 19½ pounds; the bass record, ten pounds; and a four-pound trout will win a free day ticket.

Hansen Dam, in the San Fernando Valley part of Los Angeles, is another publicly-owned reservoir, which is stocked with trout, and is virtually a neighbourhood lake. It is not known for fishing of particularly high quality, but it does provide facilities for young people in particular, without cost. Here I encountered an elderly Mexican, fishing with his grandson. The man fingered my fly line, and said to me in Spanish that it was too thick, then noticed that there was a leader attached to it, which had his approval. He had never, apparently, seen a fly line close up.

But Southern California is not without its fly-fishing enthusiasts; there is a fly-fishing association whose members are filled with enthusiasm. They press for the creation of conditions in which fly fishermen may flourish. A part of the San Gabriel River, in the mountains to the north of Los Angeles, has been stocked with trout and set aside for the exclusive use of fly fishermen. The limit is three trout, of not less than six inches. I passed this one up.

It is in the central and northern part of the state where the natural rivers and lakes produce their share of salmon and trout, and where the mighty steelhead—the sea-run rainbow—is taken. The record is 25½ pounds, caught in the Smith River, Del Norte County, on January 20, 1973.

FLY FISHING IN
NEW ZEALAND

Brown trout ova brought from Britain via Tasmania, Australia, were first successfully hatched in New Zealand in 1869. Rainbow trout ova from the Russian River in California were hatched in 1877. Both species bred swiftly and were subsequently liberated throughout the country.

In the central North Island are the lake systems of Rotorua and Taupo. Brown trout are plentiful but are greatly outnumbered by the rainbows. Being of primarily steelhead stock, the rainbows confined to the lakes are prevented from going to sea by hydro dams, but still retain steelhead characteristics. They begin their runs upstream from the lakes where they live all summer, spawn, return to the lake, and fatten up again by the autumn. Few fish stay in the streams during the summer months, December to March. Best fly fishing on streams that flow into lakes is from April onwards, when trout are running up, or in November/December when trout are dropping back to the lakes.

Brown trout predominate in the South Island, but there are also rainbow and land-locked salmon in the lake systems. Quinnat and Atlantic salmon spawn in some of the east coast rivers.

Many of the popular lakes in the South Island have hydro dams at the outlets, so, as in North Island lakes, trout run up streams during winter to spawn, returning to lakes in the summer. The hydro dams have prevented some salmon from returning to the sea and these land-locked 'Quinnats' now follow the steelhead pattern like the rainbows and browns, by living in the lake all summer and running upstream to spawn in the winter. The pattern for good fishing is similar to North Island lakes—fly fishing is best early (when trout are returning to lakes) and late in the season—April or May—when trout are beginning to run upstream to spawn.

While the North Island lakes fish well with wet fly, the southern lakes fish better with a dry fly and floating line anywhere from the lake shore.

102

The South Island rivers that run directly to the sea have resident populations of trout, mainly browns, and in some eastern rivers, Pacific salmon run in from the sea for spawning. These are the Quinnat, and runs usually start in February/March.

South Westland has one of the largest runs in the world of sea-run brown trout that come in from the sea like silver salmon to spawn in late summer, and also follow the whitebait into river mouths in the spring.

Resident browns in the rivers are mostly fished for with dry fly, and some of the finest rises in New Zealand are seen on rivers like the Mataura.

While the North Island is famous for the large rainbows of its lake systems, the South Island is usually considered the mecca for the angler who likes a small dry fly stream and quiet surroundings.

A variety of tours is available. An example is the following:

Fishing in the Rotorua Lakes District:

Within a twenty mile radius of Rotorua are eleven fishable lakes. The streams flowing into these lakes open on the 1st of December after winter spawning and close on the 30th of June. During the summer months the fish are back in the lakes. The fly fishing is predominantly wet (streamer) fly, fished with sinking lines and is done mainly at the mouths where the streams enter lakes. Chest waders are essential.

The lakes open on 1st October until 30th June, with only Lake Rotorua remaining open all year.

Popular stream mouths during the summer are the mouths of Lake Rotorua such as the Waititi, Awahaou and Hamarana, and the inlet and outlet of the Ohau Channel, the Waititi and Ruato on Lake Rotoiti and the Te Wairoa on Lake Tarawera. Many of the other good stream mouths require boat access.

For dry fly fishing, the most popular river adjacent to Rotorua is the outlet of Lake Rotoiti, the Kaituna stream, which has an excellent morning and evening rise.

However, most of the dry fly fishing is reached by car, fifty miles and more into the Urewera country to the east of Rotorua on the Waikaremoana Road. The popular easy-to-get-at streams are the Whirinaki, Rangitaiki and Whakatane. Dry or nymph fishing on these streams is best November to March. Stream mouth fishing in lakes is best in Rotorua in January, and at Tarawera in May and June, but trolling is good in all lakes from October to June. Guides are recommended, as they have boats and vehicles for access.

Recommended lines are:

A fast sinking line } Nos. 8—10
A medium sink line }

For dry fly fishing a floating line of usually Nos. 5—8.

Recommended flies are: Mrs. Simpson, Parsons' Glory, Grey Ghost, Red Setter and Hamills. Dry flies are universal, and are usually Nos. 12—16.

Best time to participate:

May & June (the best time for big rainbows—Lake Tarawera)

October to April: (during this period dry fly Urewera streams such as Rangitaika, Whakatane and Whirinaki, also fly fishing on Rotorua and the Ohau Channel)

October to June: (trolling good on all Rotorua lakes)

Number of anglers: One, two, three or four

Length of tour: six days

Day 1: Arrive Auckland International Airport and transfer to Hotel. Rest of day free.

Day 2: Transfer to Airport for scheduled flight from Auckland to Rotorua. Pick up a rental car, on arrival in Rotorua, and drive to motel. Fish afternoon.

Day 3 and 4: Fishing in and around Rotorua.

Day 5: Fishing in the morning. Fly to Auckland in afternoon and transfer to hotel in Auckland.

Day 6: Depart New Zealand.

Price of Tour:

    1 Angler . . . NZ $350.00
    2 Anglers . . . NZ $240.00 each
    3 Anglers . . . NZ $222.00 each
    4 Anglers . . . NZ $210.00 each

Price includes: Rental car with 185 miles pre-paid, internal flights, accommodations.

Price does not include: any meals, guiding services, items of a personal nature.

It is recommended that visitors to the area for the first time engage a guide at least for a day to learn of the best local methods and locations. Guides can be hired at NZ $20.00 per hour and provide all tackle, vehicle, boat, coffee, etc.

Contact: The Hunting and Fishing Officer
                   Tourist and Publicity Department
                   Private Bag
                   Rotorua, New Zealand

or   New Zealand Tourist and Publicity Department
                   New Zealand House
                   Haymarket
                   London SW1Y 4TQ

GAZETTEER OF STILL WATERS IN THE U.K.

All waters listed below offer trout fishing on a day-ticket basis. They are *fly-only* waters.

ALLEN'S FARM
Rockbourne Road, Fordingbridge, Hampshire
Tel: Rockbourne (07253) 313
March 24—October 29
5 lakes—approx 5 acres

ARDINGLEY RESERVOIR
Near Balcombe, Surrey
Tel: Forest Row (034 282) 2731
Information: Recreation Office, Weir Wood Reservoir, Forest Row, East Grinstead, Sussex
May 1—October 28
180 acres
Boats

ARDLEIGH RESERVOIR
Bookings: The Fishery Officer, Ardleigh, Colchester, Essex
Tel: (0206) 230642
April 1—October 31
130 acres
Boats

ARGAL RESERVOIR
Near Penryn, Cornwall
The Warden: Little Argal Farm, Budock, Penryn
Tel: Penryn (0326) 72544
April 1—October 12
65 acres
Boats

ARLINGTON RESERVOIR
The Lodge, Arlington, Polegate, East Sussex
Tel: (0323) 870815
April 15—October 14
120 acres
Boats

AVINGTON TROUT FISHERIES
Avington Trout Fisheries Ltd., Avington, Itchen Abbas, Winchester, Hampshire
Tel: Itchen Abbas (0962 78) 312
April 1—September 30
Three lakes

BARN ELMS No. 7
Hammersmith, London
Information: Metropolitan Water Division, New River Head, Rosebery Avenue, London EC1R 4TP
Tel: 01-837 3300 ext. 2421
March 15—November 30
23 acres

BARN ELMS No. 5
(as above)
Boat-fishing only
24 acres

THE BARROWS
(see CHEW)
April 12—October 15
26/39/60 acres

BLAGDON RESERVOIR
(see CHEW)
April 12—October 15
440 acres
Boats

BELLBROOK VALLEY FISHERY
Bellbrook, Oakford, Tiverton, Devon
Tel: Oakford (039 85) 292
March 31—December 25
Five small lakes

BEWL BRIDGE
Recreation Officer, Bewl Bridge Reservoir, Lamberhurst, Kent
Tel: Lamberhurst (089 278) 661
(Fishing Lodge, tel: (089 278) 352)
May 1—October 28
770 acres
Boats

CAMELEY TROUT LAKES
Hillcrest Farm, Cameley, Temple Cloud, near Bristol
Tel: (0761) 52423
April 1—October 15
Two lakes—2¼ and 1½ acres

CHEW RESERVOIR
Information: Bristol Waterworks Company, Recreations Dept.
Woodford Lodge, Chew Stoke, Bristol
Tel: Chew Stoke (02 7589) 2339
April 12—October 15
1200 acres
Boats

CHURCH HILL FARM
Mursley, Bucks
Tel: (029 672) 524
April 1—September 30
Two lakes—7 acres/2½ acres

CLATWORTHY RESERVOIR
Near Wiveliscombe, Somerset
Tel: (0984) 23549
March 31—October 15
130 acres
Boats

DAMERHAM
Damerham South End, Fordingbridge, Hampshire
Tel: Rockbourne (072 53) 446
April 1—October 31
Five lakes—17 acres

DARWELL RESERVOIR
Near Mountfield, Robertsbridge, Sussex
Tel: Robertsbridge (0580) 880 407
180 acres
April 1—October 29
Boats

DERWENT RESERVOIR
Edmundbyers, Co. Durham
Sunderland and South Shields Water Company, 29 John Street, Sunderland
Tel: Sunderland (0783) 57123
May 1—October 14
1,000 acres
Boats

DRAYCOTE WATER
Kites Hardwick, near Rugby
Tel: Rugby (0788) 811107
April 13—October 20
600 acres
Boats

DURLEIGH
Near Bridgwater, Somerset
Tel: Bridgwater (0278) 4786
March 24—October 15
80 acres
Boats

ELINOR TROUT FISHERIES
Aldwinkle Northamptonshire
40 North Street, Oundle, Peterborough
Tel: Oundle (083 22) 3671
April 1—October 31
36 acres
Punts

EYE BROOK RESERVOIR
Corby, Northamptonshire
Tel: Rockingham (053 670) 770 264
March 30—September 30
400 acres
Boats

FARMOOR II RESERVOIR
Farmoor, near Oxford
Vales Division, Thames Water Authority, Denton House, Iffley Turn,
Oxford OX4 4HJ
Tel: Oxford (0865) 778921, or Gatehouse: Cumnor (086 76) 3033
April 1—November 30
240 acres

FERNWORTHY
Near Chagford, Devon
South West Water Authority, 3-5 Barnfield Road, Exeter, Devon
Tel: Exeter (0392) 31666
April 1—October 12
76 acres
Boats

FEWSTON
North Yorkshire
Information: Yorkshire Water Authority
Tel: Leeds (0532) 448201/Harrogate (0423) 64466
March 25—September 30
156 Acres

FLOWERS FARM LAKES
Hilfield, Batcombe Down, Dorchester, Dorset
Tel: Cerne Abbas (030 03) 351
April 1—October 15
2 acres

FOREMARK RESERVOIR
Leicester Water Centre, Gorse Hill, Anstey, Leicestershire
Tel: Anstey (053 721) 352011
May 4—October 15
230 acres
Boats

GRAFHAM WATER
Bedford Water Division, Grafham Water Area, West Perry, Huntingdon, Cambridgeshire
Tel: Huntingdon (0480) 810531
April 28—October 28
1,500 acres
Boats

GREAT SANDERS RESERVOIR
Sedlescombe, Sussex
Tel: Sedlescombe (042 487) 248
April 1—October 29
54 acres
Boats

HILL VIEW TROUT LAKE
19 St. Leonard's Drive, Chapel St. Leonard's, near Skegness, Lincolnshire
Tel: Skegness (0754) 72979
April 1—October 28
2 acres

JOHN O'GAUNT'S LAKE
How Park Farm, King's Somborne, Stockbridge, Hampshire
Tel: King's Somborne (079 47) 353
April 1—October 14
5 acres

KENNICK
'Yonder', Whitstone Lane, Bovey Tracey, Devon
Tel: Bovey Tracey (0626) 833199
April 1—October 12
45 acres

LADYBOWER RESERVOIR
Severn-Trent Water Authority, Bamford, near Sheffield
Tel: Bamford (043 34) 424/254
April 7—October 15
500 acres
Boats

LARTINGTON HIGH LAKE
Riversdale, Lartington, Co. Durham
Tel: Cotherstone (08335) 632
April 1—October 31
9½ acres

LATIMER PARK LAKES
Latimer, near Chesham, Bucks.
Tel: Little Chalfont (024 04) 2386
April 2—September 30
Two lakes—12 acres
Boats

LEOMINSTEAD TROUT FISHERY
Emery Down, Lyndhurst, Hampshire
Tel: Lyndhurst (042 128) 2610
April 1—October 31
8 acres

LINACRE RESERVOIR
Severn-Trent Water Authority, Dimple Road, Matlock, Derbys.
Tel: Matlock (0629) 55051
April 1—September 30
44 acres

LINCH HILL FISHERY
Stanton Harcourt, Near Eynsham, Oxfordshire
Tel: (086 731) 774
April 1—October 31
Two lakes: 58 acres and 12 acres
Boats

LITTLE HEATH FARM
Gamlingay, Bedfordshire
Tel: Gamlingay (0767) 50301
April 21—October 31
6 acres

LOWER MOOR FISHERY
Oaksey, Malmesbury, Wiltshire
Tel: Minety (066 640) 232
April 1—October 31
Two lakes—30 acres and 7 acres

NARBOROUGH LAKES
Narborough, King's Lynn, Norfolk
Tel: (07603) 292
April 2—October 28
Two small lakes

NETHERHALL TROUT FISHERY
Crown Fishery, Carthagena Lock, Broxbourne, Herts.
Tel: Hoddesdon 61048
April 1—September 30
6 acres

OGSTON RESERVOIR
Severn-Trent Water Authority, Dimple Road, Matlock, Derbyshire
Tel: Matlock (0629) 55051
April 1—October 15
203 acres

OUGHTON TROUT FISHERY
Burford Trout Farm, Ickleford, nr. Hitchin, Herts.
Tel: Hitchin (0462) 4201 or 52855
April 1—October 31
2¾ acres

PACKINGTON FISHERIES
near Meriden, Coventry, West Midlands
Tel: Meriden (0676) 22754
March 18—November 15
87 acres
Boats

PEATSWOOD LAKES
Broomhall Lodge, Peatswood, Market Drayton, Shropshire
Tel: Market Drayton (0630) 4505 or 3222
March 15—November 15
Two lakes—5½ and 2½ acres
Boats

PITSFORD RESERVOIR
Northampton Water Division, Cliftonville, Northampton
Tel: Northampton (0604) 21321
April 1—October 28
739 acres
Boats

THE POOH CORNER FISHERY
Near Rolvenden, Cranbrook, Kent
Tel: (058 084) 219
April 3—October 31
2 acres

PORTH RESERVOIR
Newquay, Cornwall
Tel: Newquay (063 73) 2701
April 1—October 2
40 acres
Boats

QUEEN MOTHER RESERVOIR
Recreation Centre, Horton Road, Colnbrook, Slough
Tel: Colnbrook 4126
April 1—November 30
475 acres
Boats only

RIVER FARM TROUT FISHERY
Titchfield, Hampshire
Tel: Titchfield (032 94) 41215
April 1—October 29
2½ acres

RUTLAND WATER
The Fishing Lodge, Whitwell, Oakham, Leicestershire
Tel: Empingham (078 086) 770
April 27—October 28
3,000 acres
Boats

SIBLYBACK LAKE
Tregarrick Lodge, Common Moor, St. Cleer, Liskeard, Cornwall
Tel: Liskeard (0579) 42410
April 1—October 12
140 acres
Boats

STAFFORD MOOR
Dolton, Winkleigh, N. Devon
Tel: Dolton (080 54) 371
April 10—October 10
14 acres

STITHIANS RESERVOIR
Stithians, Cornwall
Information: South West Water Authority, 3-5 Barnfield Road, Exeter, Devon
Tel: Exeter (0392) 31666
March 15—October 12
274 acres

SUTTON BINGHAM
Near Yeovil, Somerset
Tel: (0935) 872389
March 26—October 15
142 acres
Boats

(UPPER) TAMAR
near Kilkhampton, Cornwall
Tel: Kilkhampton (028 882) 262
April 1—October 12
81 acres
Boats

TENTERDEN TROUT WATERS
Coombe Farm, Tenterden, Kent
Tel: Tenterden (05806) 3201
April 1—October 31
3 acres

THORNTON RESERVOIR
Information: Leicester Water Centre, Gorse Hill, Anstey, Leicestershire
Tel: Anstey (053 721) 352011
March 28—October 15
76 acres
Boats

THRUSCROSS RESERVOIR
(See FEWSTON)
142 acres

THURSTONFIELD LOUGH
Lough House, Thurstonfield, Carlisle, Cumbria
Tel: Burgh by Sands (022 876) 431
March 15—October 15
37 acres
Boats

TITTESWORTH RESERVOIR
Leek, Staffordshire
Severn-Trent Water Authority, Westport Road, Burslem , Stoke
Tel: 053 834 389 or 0782 85601
April 7—October 15
190 acres
Boats

TOFT NEWTON RESERVOIR
Anglian Water Authority, Lincolnshire River Division, 50 Wide Bargate, Boston, Lincolnshire
Tel: Boston (0205) 65661
April 13—October 29
40 acres

TOTTIFORD
(see KENNICK)
35 acres

TRENCHFORD
(see KENNICK)
33 acres

WALTHAMSTOW No. 4
Walthamstow, London
Metropolitan Water Division, New River Head, Rosebery Avenue,
London EC1R 4TP
Tel: 01-837 3300 ext 2421
April 8—November 30
30 acres

WHALLEY ABBEY RESERVOIR
Clitheroe, Lancashire
Tel: Whalley (025 482) 2151
April 1—September 30
7 acres

WILLINGHURST TROUT FISHERY
Shamley Green, Guildford, Surrey
Tel: Cranleigh (04866) 2828 or 3739
April 1—November 18
Four lakes—6 acres

WISTLANDPOUND RESERVOIR
Bratton Flemming, Barnstaple, Devon
South West Water Authority, 3-5 Barnfield Road, Exeter, Devon
Tel: Exeter (0392) 3166
April 1—October 12
41 acres

WROUGHTON RESERVOIR
Wroughton, Swindon, Wiltshire
Cotswold Division, Thames Water Authority, 17 Bath Road, Swindon, SN1 4AT
Tel: Swindon (0793) 24331
April 1—November 30
3 acres
Punts

WALES

BEACON'S RESERVOIR
Llwyn-on near Merthyr Tydfil
Tel: Merthyr Tydfil (0685) 5457
March 21—September 30
52 acres

BRENIG RESERVOIR
Corwen, Clwyd.
Llyn Brenig Information Centre, Cerrig-y-Drudion, Corwen
Tel: Cerrig-y-Drudion (049 082) 463
April 1—October 15
919 acres
Boats

CAMBRIAN FISHERIES
Near Afonwen, Mold, Clwyd
Tel:, (03528) 589
March 7—November 25
18 acres
Boats

LISVANE RESERVOIR
Cardiff, South Glamorgan
Tel: Cardiff (0222) 752238
March 21—September 30
19 acres

LLANDEGFEDD RESERVOIR
Panteg, near Pontypool, Gwent
April 4—October 14
429 acres
Boats

LLANISHEN RESERVOIR
(see LISVANE)
59 acres

LLANLLAWDDOG LAKE
Home Farm, Llanllawddog, Carmarthen, Dyfed.
Tel: Llanpumsaint (026 784) 436
March 10—September 30
2½ acres

(UPPER) LLIEDI RESERVOIR
Swiss Valley, Llanelli, Dyfed.
Tel: Llanelli (055 42) 3031
April 4—September 30
34 acres
Boats

LLWYN-ON RESERVOIR
Near Merthyr Tydfil, Mid-Glamorgan
Tel: Merthyr Tydfil (0685) 5457
March 21—September 30
150 acres
Boats

(LOWER) NEUADD RESERVOIR
Pont-sticill, near Merthyr Tydfil, Mid-Glamorgan
Tel: Merthyr Tydfil (0685) 2404
March 21—September 30
12 acres

(UPPER) NEUADD RESERVOIR
(See LOWER NEUADD RESERVOIR)
57 acres

LLYN-Y-TARW
Newtown, Powys
Information: The Sports Shop, Shortbridge Street, Newtown, Powys
Tel: Newtown (0686) 26917
March 18—October 15
10 acres

LAKE VYRNWY
Lake Vyrnwy Hotel, Llanwddyn, Powys.
Tel: Llanwddyn (069 173) 244
March 1—October 14
1,100 acres
Boats

WENTWOOD RESERVOIR
Llanvaches, Penhow, Newport, Gwent
Tel: Penhow (063 345) 213
April 4—October 14
41 acres
Boats

SCOTLAND

ACREKNOWE RESERVOIR
Stotharts, 6 High Street, Hawick, Roxburghshire
Tel: Hawick (0450) 3349
March 15—September 30

ARTLOCH DEVERONSIDE FISHERIES
Tourist Board Office, Huntly, Aberdeenshire
Tel: Huntly (0466) 3448
March 1—October 31
5 acres

CAMERON RESERVOIR
St. Andrews Angling Club, 54 St Nicholas Street, St. Andrews, Fife
Tel: Peat Inn (033 484) 236
April 15—September 30

COLDINGHAM LOCH
Coldingham Village, Berwickshire
Tel: Coldingham (03903) 270
22 acres
March 15—October 29
Boats

DUNALASTAIR RESERVOIR
nr. Tummel Bridge
Dunalastair Hotel, Kinloch Rannoch, Perthshire
Tel: Kinloch Rannoch (088 22) 323
March 15—October 6
Boats

DALBEATTIE RESERVOIR
Dalbeattie Angling Association, 30 High Street, Dalbeattie, Kircudbrightshire
April 15—September 30

DINDINNIE RESERVOIR
Stranraer & District Angling Association, Larg Road, Stranraer, Wigtownshire
Tel: Stranraer (0776) 3312
March 15—September 30

FRUID RESERVOIR
nr. Moffat, Dumfries & Galloway
Lothian Regional Council, Dept. of Water Supply Services, Comiston Springs, 55 Buckstone Terrace, Edinburgh
Tel: 031-445 4141
Boats

GLENFARG RESERVOIR
nr. Bridge of Earn
Regional Water Engineer, Fife & Kinross Water Board, Flemington Road, Glenrothes, Fife
Tel: Glenrothes (0592) 756541
April 1—September 30

GLENKILN RESERVOIR
Director of Water and Sewerage, Dumfries and Galloway Regional Council, 70 Terregles Street, Dumfries
Tel: Dumfries (0387) 63011
April 1—September 30

MONIKIE RESERVOIR
nr. Muirdrum
Water Services Dept. 101 Ward Road, Dundee, Fife
Tel: Dundee (0382) 21164
April 10—September 25
Boats

WATCH RESERVOIR
Rathburne Hotel, Longformacus, Berwickshire
March 15—September 30
Boats

WHITEADDER RESERVOIR
nr. Gifford
Water Engineer, Aldeston House, Haddington, East Lothian
Tel: Haddington (062 082) 4131
April 15—September 30
Boats